ORGANIZING
IDEA BOOK

ORGANIZING
IDEA BOOK

JOHN LOECKE

The Taunton Press

The Taunton Press, Inc., 63 South Main Street, PO Box 5506, Newtown, CT 06470-5506
e-mail: tp@taunton.com

EDITOR: Jennifer Matlack
INTERIOR DESIGN AND LAYOUT: Jeanette Leendertse
ILLUSTRATOR: Christine Erickson
FRONT COVER PHOTOGRAPHERS:
    Top row, left to right: Photo © Wendell T. Webber; Photo © Rob Karosis; Photo © Wendell T.
    Webber; Photo © Erik Piasecki
    Middle row, left to right: Photo © Phillip Ennis; Photo © Melabee M. Miller; Photo © Brian Vanden Brink,
    Photographer 2005; Photo by John Rickard © The Taunton Press, Inc.
    Bottom row, left to right: Photo © Wendell T. Webber; Photo © Wendell T. Webber; Photo © Mark Samu;
    Photo © Melabee M. Miller
BACK COVER PHOTOGRAPHERS: Top: Photo © Wendell T. Webber; Bottom, left to right: Photo © Alise O'Brien;
    Photo © Brian Vanden Brink, Photographer 2005; Photo © Wendell T. Webber

Taunton Home® is a trademark of The Taunton Press, Inc.,
registered in the U.S. Patent and Trademark Office.

Library of Congress Cataloging-in-Publication Data
Loecke, John.
  Organizing idea book / John Loecke.
     p. cm.
  ISBN-13: 978-1-56158-780-3
  ISBN-10: 1-56158-780-X
  1. Interior decoration. 2. Storage in the home. I. Title.
  NK2115.L79 2005
  747--dc22
                              2005015196

Printed in the United States of America
10 9 8 7 6 5 4 3

The following manufacturers/names appearing in *Organizing Idea Book* are trademarks: Bed Bath & Beyond®, Better Homes
and Gardens®, California Closets®, Casabella®, ClosetMaid®, The Container Store®, Exposures®, Filofax®, Freedom Bag®,
Frontgate®, Ikea®, Kmart™, Levenger®, NARI®, Rev-A-Shelf®, Rubbermaid®, Stacks and Stacks™, Target®, Tupperware®,

Acknowledgments

THIS BOOK WOULD NOT HAVE BEEN POSSIBLE without the support of many people. First, thank you to Peter Lemos for introducing me to The Taunton Press. Peter, without your introduction, this book would not have been possible. Thanks also to Carolyn Mandarano and Jennifer Matlack, my editors. Carolyn and Jennifer, you worked around my hectic schedule to help me pull this book together and for that I am truly grateful. Thanks also to Wendell T. Webber, Joshua McHugh, Melabee M. Miller, and all of the many other photographers whose work provides the context for my words. I'm grateful to Jason Oliver Nixon for turning a blind eye when our dining room table became my office, rendering dinner parties impossible for months on end. And finally, to my parents, Ray and Marlene Loecke, for teaching me everything I know about maintaining a well-ordered home.

Contents

Introduction

When I mentioned to friends and family that I was writing a book on organizing, I was greeted with silence. Then came the jokes and the ribbing. Would writing such a book empty my apartment of the dozens of Chinese figurines that fill my many bookshelves? How could someone who couldn't bear to part with piles of old decorating magazines enlighten others on the art of order?

Simple, I replied, because for me, a well-ordered home has always been an obsession. And, yes, my Chinoiserie stands at perfect attention and my magazines are boxed and labeled. Organization is a topic that I've both studied extensively and practiced professionally, both in my career as an interior designer and in my work as a contributing home editor to a number of national magazines, including *Parents*® and *Better Homes and Gardens*®.

But obsessed though I may be with the art of organizing, I did feel the need for additional backup as I wrote this book. And what I learned from talking to friends and experts such as Jill Markiewicz, the owner of Closet Couture, a high-style New York-based organizing service, and Lyn Peterson, an interior designer, mother of four, and all-around organizing guru, was that many of us (myself included) avoid tackling organizing projects because we know things will only get worse before they get better. But that's simply how the process works, and once you've accepted that, the rest is easy.

I also discovered that organizing is a process and not one that requires you to tackle the entire house in one sweeping session. For this reason, you'll find that this book is arranged according to the various hot spots in the home, starting with the area inside the front door and continuing through to the garage. So if you're obsessed with closets as I am (I've not only said good riddance to wire hangers, but I've also coordinated the contents of mine by color), you'll know right where to look.

What are you waiting for? Get organized!

The Ins and Outs of Organizing

Getting organized means different things to different people. For some, it's a call to pare down possessions and donate anything that's no longer needed to charity. For others, it means adding things like a sturdy set of shelves so that a collection of books has a permanent place to reside. Then there are those who are somewhere in between. They see the organizing process as both adding and subtracting—a chance to reduce and renew while making their home a more enjoyable place to live. For others still, organizing is a chance to rethink how they live, what they keep, and how they keep it.

But no matter what organizing means to you, chances are it has the same gratifying effect: It makes you feel good. Just think of the feeling of satisfaction that washes over you after you've accomplished even the smallest organizing feat, like cleaning out your purse or briefcase. Putting things in order has the uncanny ability to make us think a little clearer and breathe a little easier.

THE BIG PICTURE

Before you donate long-forgotten items to charity or buy a new chest of drawers to store out-of-season clothing or gear, stop for a moment. Step back and consider your

◀ A WELL-ORDERED HOME STARTS AT THE FRONT DOOR. Here, a sturdy bench provides a place to rest while putting on or taking off shoes; cubbies, one for each member of the family, organize coats, hats, and other outdoor gear.

▶ WIRE RACKS LIKE THE ONES shown here are one of the many tools available for maximizing shelf space and improving the functionality of your kitchen cabinets.

▼ AN ALTERNATIVE TO CLASSIC PEGBOARD, a tongue and groove panel system that accepts wire baskets and hooks is ideal for organizing tools and garden gear.

whole house, not just one room or area. By contemplating the bigger picture before adding or subtracting things, you can be assured that you won't later regret giving away those red corduroy pants that you never wear but still adore. You'll also save yourself from getting rid of seemingly useless items that, with a little creative thinking, can actually serve a useful purpose. For instance, those old metal bicycle baskets may appear as piles of junk in your garage, but clean them off and hang them on the bathroom wall and you've got yourself a few sturdy, albeit eclectic, baskets for storing toiletries, towels, even magazines.

ASSESS THE SITUATION

Assessing the larger situation at hand requires that you see your home—and all of its clutter—in a new way. To help you be objective, grab a pad of paper and a pen, and survey each room. Pretend you're a stranger and write down the things in each space that need improvement. Are there too many coats piled in the front foyer? Does the dining room table serve as a dumping ground for mail? Do you have to push a pile of clothes off the bed before you can climb into it at night? These are the types of questions you must ask yourself as you move from room to room.

Performing this often-overlooked step at the start will ensure that you create an organizing plan that fits your lifestyle. For example, if mail does pile up on the dining room table and there's no way to get around that, perhaps you can outfit the table with an attractive basket that can corral the envelopes and magazines. Then when you want to use the room for dining, cleaning off the table is easy—simply remove the basket and the table is ready to be set. Or,

▲ **IF THE ENTRANCE YOUR FAMILY USES** every day opens into your kitchen, follow this homeowner's lead and convert a pair of base cabinets into locker-style cubbies for coats, bags, and other outdoor gear. Pull-out baskets, which would normally be used for storing vegetables, can accommodate hats, gloves, and scarves.

▲ CABINETS ARE ESSENTIAL organizing tools. Here, they help maintain order in this utility room, offering open shoe cubbies and closed-door types for supplies; a message board makes it easy to track when supplies are running low.

if clothes tend to get heaped on your bed, perhaps installing pegs or hooks on the bedroom wall or on the back of the closet door will provide additional space for your wardrobe. The important thing to remember is that getting organized isn't about changing the way you live, but rather it's about accommodating your lifestyle.

If you're still unsure about why you should create lasting order in your home, consider the person who decides to clean his closet. Before he makes a full assessment of his wardrobe, he typically rushes to the store and stocks up on hangers, shoe boxes, garment bags, and other organizational gear. Three months later, the closet is in complete disarray again. Why? Because he never took the time to fully evaluate the situation and consequently stocked up on storage supplies that, in the end, only added to the mess. Sure, the right gear is important, but perhaps every article of clothing doesn't belong on a hanger. Perhaps shirts should be hanging and pants would be better kept folded on shelves. Bottom line: Think before you buy. Don't stock up on organizing

▶ A CLOSET BECOMES INSTANTLY UNORGANIZED when hangers get jumbled together. Replace all wire hangers with plastic-coated types to keep clothes hung straight and separate.

▼ AN ADJUSTABLE SHELVING SYSTEM will improve the inner workings of any closet. In this kitchen space they help keep pans, canned goods, and other cooking gear in order.

▲ WHEN PLACED NEAR A STOVE or cooktop, a narrow pullout cabinet is the perfect place to stow spatulas, ladles, and other utensils, freeing valuable counter space.

▼ PERFECT FOR SMALL SPACES, a cabinet or armoire can be outfitted to accommodate an alternate use. Here, door-mounted baskets keep current projects close at hand, while magnetized containers keep essential supplies like paper clips and rubber bands tidy.

► WHETHER YOU'RE STOWING office supplies in your desk or socks in a dresser, the rule of thumb is to group like items in smaller containers. Here, a compartmentalized tray keeps desktop essentials orderly.

supplies without getting real about how you live or what you really need to keep.

PLAN YOUR ATTACK

Once you've completed your walk-through, establish a plan of attack. If you're the type who is easily distracted or has difficulty prioritizing, take a step back and give everything on your list a stress rating (a number from 1 to 10, with 10 being the most worrisome) that indicates the extent to which the problem in question bothers you. For example, if your kitchen scores a 10, then that's where you should focus your energy—the bedroom, bathroom, and garage will simply have to wait.

Start Small

Tackling the biggest project first may seem overwhelming, but don't let the process get the best of you. The key to organizing any space is simply getting started. And to do that, you need only take your first small step. So while all of the corners of your kitchen may be screaming for your attention, focus on one pint-sized area. Begin with the junk drawer, for example. After

◄ **LIMITING THE AMOUNT** of floor storage in a small bathroom will help the room feel larger and more tidy. If you go this route, be sure to use wall space wisely, enlisting the aid of multiple towel racks and shelving over the sink.

emptying the contents and discarding dried-out pens, dead batteries, expired coupons, and other things you no longer need, examine what remains. Group like items, then outfit the drawer with plastic, metal, or wire bins that are sized to fit what you have to store. The bins will not only help you maintain order, but they also will make it possible to find what you need fast. Or start even smaller: Free up precious drawer space by moving your table linens from a kitchen drawer to a basket that can be set on a shelf next to the dining room table. This will give you extra room for storing utensils or other cooking items and put napkins and table-cloths where you need them most.

Others problems, like establishing a place for everything in a kitchen that has only a handful of cupboards, will require more of an investment—both emotionally and

monetarily. But once you begin to solve smaller organizing issues, you'll be ready to dive into these bigger challenges. If you simply can't pare down your china or cookware, for instance, you may have to augment the existing storage by adding a freestanding cupboard or island. If your counter is over-run with cookbooks, leaving you no place to work, you may need to clean out a cabinet or add a sturdy set of shelves. Don't forget: What matters is not how much you have left to do but that you're making progress!

RULES TO LIVE BY

Whether you're beginning your journey to a more organized way of living by tackling small spaces one at a time or reworking every room in your house at once, keep the following guidelines in mind:

▶ WHAT'S THE SECRET to getting kids to put away their belongings? Implement an easy-to-follow storage system and label everything with words and pictures. The bins that help keep this armoire tidy are painted with chalkboard paint and labeled with chalk so markings can be easily changed.

• **Storage and organizing go hand in hand.** What's more, good storage saves steps. Strive to stow things where they're used, and group them by task or activity. For example, the best place to keep soup ladles, spatulas, and other cooking utensils is near the stovetop. Also avoid forcing yourself to learn new habits. If shoes are always piling up by the door, create storage for them there by adding a large bin or basket.

• **The more often you use something, the more accessible it should be.** Items you use everyday, like car and house keys, should be at your fingertips. Items you use a couple of times a month, like files for sorting bills, should be fairly easy to reach. Things that are used once a year, like holiday decorations, are best kept in out-of-the-way places like garages, basements, or attics.

• **When packing things away, never underestimate the power of a good-looking label.** It can spare you the hassle of digging through unmarked boxes. More important, well-labeled shelves and containers help everyone in your household remember at a glance where things belong. Another idea: Photograph each container's contents and tape the image to the box. This visual inventory will make things less likely to go astray.

• **You don't have to spend a lot—or even any—money to get yourself more organized.** Instead, tap into your home's hidden poten-

tial. Empty existing closets of things you no longer use. Repeat the process with bookshelves and cabinets. The spare spaces you uncover may be all the room you need to get your home life in order.

• **Don't skimp.** While saving money is a good thing, make sure that the ways you go about cutting costs don't end up cramping your lifestyle. For example, if you love to cook but don't because your kitchen is a recipe for disaster, spend the money to make it better. Add extra shelves to cabinets, or even add extra cabinets, so you can easily find the things you need.

• **Understand that it's okay to ask for help.** If the thought of emptying your closets of their contents, sorting through everything, and placing it all back in an orderly fashion has your head spinning, know that there are professionals who can help by assessing your situation and devising a plan of attack. To find one in your area, contact the National

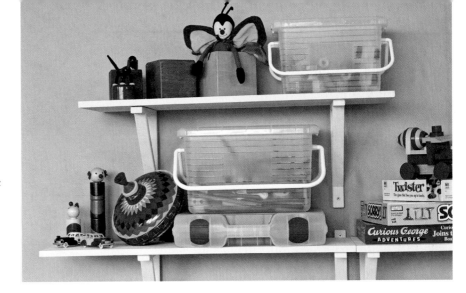

Association of Professional Organizers by logging on to www.napo.net, or look under Professional Organizers in the Yellow Pages of your local phone book.

▲ YOU DON'T HAVE TO SPEND a lot of money to organize your child's belongings. Here, simple wood shelves get toys off the floor. Plastic bins with handles for easy toting hold playthings, like buildings blocks, that have multiple pieces.

KEEPING ORDER

While it's true that a well-organized home is easy to maintain, doing so requires that you do a little each day in order to stay on track. Spend 15 minutes going through the mail when you get home each night. And keep two piles, one for magazines and catalogs and another for bills and letters; go through the catalogs once a week and recycle what you don't want. You'll maintain order, too, if you put things away as soon as you're finished using them. For example, if you've finished with a library book, place it in a bag by your door rather than in a pile in the living room. This way, when you head out to work, you can grab the bag and return the book on your way home. Every month, tackle a particular room in your home. And twice a year, schedule a major cleaning.

Organizing is a skill, not a talent. With a little forethought and some effort on your part, you can regain control of your life— not to mention find those house keys you've misplaced once again.

▲ THE MORE OFTEN you use something, the more accessible it should be. Because the owner of this kitchen likes to entertain, platters, trays, and other serving items are kept in the open.

Entryways

I f your home is like most, you probably have to step over a pile of coats and bags to get through the front door. It's a common problem of such high-traffic areas. However, with a little organization, it's possible to turn a clogged entry into space that says "welcome home" every time you pass through it. Plus, you want to greet visitors and guests with a good first impression, not a cluttered mess. Pretty is important, but practical is better.

With a little creative thinking, you can transform this space with furniture and accessories you already have. A chest of drawers, for example, can become a landing spot for car keys and the day's mail as well as storage for seasonal items such as hats and gloves. With the addition of a lower shelf, a bench not only becomes a place to take off shoes but also a place to stow them. If floor space is limited, take advantage of the surrounding walls. Peg boards and hooks require little room and can get most anything off the floor and out of the way. And whatever you do, don't forget the kids. If you want them to put away their belongings the moment they walk in the door, make sure it's convenient for them to do so.

◄ A STAIR TREAD EXTENDED around the corner of the staircase creates a handy built-in bench in this entry. Although it would have been easier and less expensive simply to add a seat, this clever design not only creates cohesiveness between two distinct spaces but also adds architectural interest.

Outerwear and Outdoor Gear

WHETHER YOUR HOME'S PRIMARY PLACE of entry is a formal front hall or a casual mudroom, without the right organization plan, the space will become piled with coats, shoes, bags, and other daily essentials. Although corralling clutter behind a closet door is ideal, it's not always the most practical solution—especially when you factor in the number of times that you and your family pass through this space each day, needing the very things that are shut away. A better plan is to have organized storage out in the open where it is easily accessible morning through night. A custom built-in unit with hooks, pegs, and open shelves, for instance, will make reaching for a jacket on brisk mornings or cool evenings an effortless task.

▲ NO CLOSET REQUIRED. An alcove, like the one shown here, will easily organize gear. Simply outfit the space with hooks and shelves as you would a closet. To maximize the space, stack hooks vertically in rows; just be sure to measure first so the coats on the highest row don't cover those below.

◄ SEATING IS A USEFUL ADDITION to any foyer, providing a place to rest while lacing up boots and shoes. By adding a shelf below this built-in bench, the owners created two levels of storage, preventing footwear from piling up haphazardly on the floor.

◄ NO MUDROOM? No worries. An upholstered bench with built-in cubbies—and smaller matching wall unit—easily accommodates all types of indoor and outdoor gear. In lieu of traditional rubber boot trays, use metal cookie sheets to protect rugs or carpets from mud and moisture.

▼ EVEN THE SMALLEST OF SPACES, like the nook to the left of this door, can be made more efficient. All that's required are a few hooks and a bench that's sized to fit the space. Covering the floor with linoleum is ideal since it's easy to wipe up on wet days.

THE PROS KNOW

Transform your foyer into a more functional space with the following furnishings:

- A mirror lets you check your appearance before heading out the door.
- A bench provides a resting place while putting on or taking off shoes. Those with seats that lift up offer the added benefit of additional storage.
- An armoire stores out-of-season clothing and gear when closet space is limited.
- A chest or table serves as a temporary resting place for mail, packages, and keys.

Mudroom Basics

Converting a side or back entrance into a full-fledged mudroom will go a long way toward preventing pile-ups by your front door. Of course, the larger your entry, the more options you'll have, but even small spaces can contain a mudroom. Here's what to include:

- A closet, armoire, or built-in cabinet that can be used to store seasonal outerwear
- Baskets or bins for sports equipment
- Shelves to raise book bags, boxes, and other large items off the floor
- A bench or chair for changing shoes
- Bins for incoming and outgoing mail
- Hooks or containers for keys
- A stand for umbrellas
- Pegs or hooks for coats, jackets, and hats
- A resilient floor such as linoleum or vinyl that's easy to clean
- Waterproof containers for wet clothing

And if you have a pet, don't forget:
- Hooks for leashes
- A pet door
- Storage for food
- Space for a dog bed or sleeping quarters

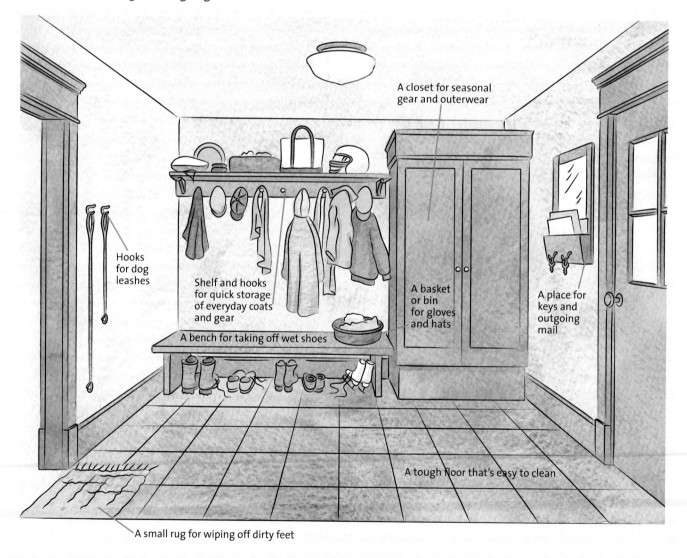

Hooks for dog leashes

Shelf and hooks for quick storage of everyday coats and gear

A bench for taking off wet shoes

A closet for seasonal gear and outerwear

A basket or bin for gloves and hats

A place for keys and outgoing mail

A tough floor that's easy to clean

A small rug for wiping off dirty feet

▲ AN ALTERNATIVE TO TRADITIONAL CLOSETS, locker-style built-ins have the added advantage of being open and easy to reach—a plus where kids are concerned. If space permits, provide one section for each member of your family.

▲ THIS NARROW MUDROOM is put to best use with a simple built-in with drawers. The same effect could be achieved with stacked storage cubes or ready-to-assemble cabinets.

◄ PEGS AND HOOKS are perhaps one of the easiest organizing tools available today. They make the most of this small apartment entryway.

A Foyer for All Seasons

Keep your front entry tidy by following these suggestions for handling the gear needed for different types of weather.

Cold Weather

- Keep only in-season coats, jackets, scarves, and hats in the closet or near the entryway door.

- If you're using hooks and pegs, designate one spot for each family member so that one person's items are all together.

- Keep hats and gloves in the sleeve of a coat to keep them from ending up on the floor (or on the wrong person!).

Warm Weather

- Replace the umbrella stand with a receptacle for sports equipment and other outdoor gear.
- Pack a bag for the beach or park and leave it in the hall closet.
- Hang bike helmets and baseball caps by the straps so they stay put.

Wet Weather

- Change a decorative doormat to a more rugged style that can easily handle heavy, messy boots.

- Leave a basket of old bath towels by the door in case a guest, family member, or pet needs to dry off when he comes inside.

- Set out a galvanized metal tray or several cookie sheets to collect wet boots and shoes.

▲ A ROW OF STURDY HOOKS and a simple bench ease the transition between indoors and out. A nearby walk-in closet with a wall of built-ins provides hidden but easily accessible storage for hats, gloves, and other gear.

▲ STORAGE DOESN'T HAVE TO STAND OUT. Instead, make it an extension of the architecture of the space. In this mudroom, the coat pegs, made from the same wood used to frame the door, blend into the room. A covered bench is a practical solution for hiding gear that's not in season.

◄ IF THE DOOR YOUR FAMILY REGULARLY USES leads from the driveway or garage to the kitchen, convert a pantry-style cabinet into open storage for outdoor items. After removing the doors, line the shelves with wicker baskets. Add a row of hooks for jackets, bike helmets, even cloth shopping bags.

◀ PRACTICAL CAN BE GOOD-LOOKING. Line the walls of your mudroom with open cubbies sized to fit all types of things you use when heading in or out the door. Hooks make it easy to put coats and umbrellas away quickly while benches provide ample space to spread out. A stone floor is a practical choice for easy cleanup.

Be Creative with the Ordinary

Sometimes the best storage solutions are right under your nose. For example, this laundry sorter embellished with appliquéd sports balls finds new purpose as an organizer for everything from hockey sticks to footballs. Other everyday items can assist you in your organizing efforts. Here are a few useful ideas:

- Hang a canvas shoe organizer on the back of a closet door and use the pockets to store hats and gloves during the winter.

- Stash summer gear in mesh laundry bags. This way, you won't have to hunt for towels, toys, or sunscreen when it's time to head to the beach. Instead, you can simply grab your bag and go.

- Use an accordion-style drying rack to keep scarves in order.

▶ FIND NEW USES FOR OLD EQUIPMENT. Here, a wheeled laundry sorter is used to corral sports gear. When not in use, simply roll the cart into a nearby closet.

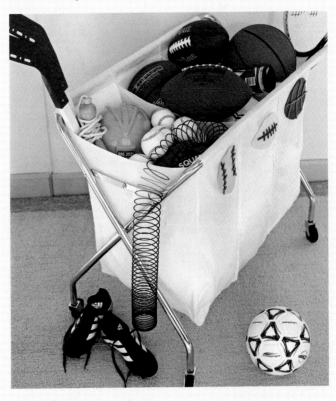

Information Centers

AN ENTRY CAN BE MORE THAN A PLACE to welcome guests and collect coats. With the right storage pieces, it can also double as a message and mail-sorting center as well as a place to stockpile essential supplies like flashlights, batteries, and spare keys. An appropriately sized chest or console, for example, can serve all of these functions. Or you can forgo furniture altogether. The area beneath a staircase or an empty wall adjacent to the front door can be converted to usable storage with the addition of shelves or built-ins. Even the back of a closet door can be transformed into practical space: Adding a bulletin board or chalkboard makes it a family message center.

▲ WHAT'S THE EASIEST WAY to create a family message center? Mount a chalk or dry erase board over the place where everyone keeps their coats.

▲ A MESSAGE CENTER can be as simple as a wall-hung basket. Here, the basket is hanging from a coat rack, doubling the usefulness of this narrow entrance.

◀ A HALL TABLE provides plenty of surface area for setting mail and packages, but a cabinet with doors and drawers can be more practical—especially if you outfit the drawers with store-bought bins. Sized to hold keys, tape, and other small items, bins will keep clutter off the table top.

▲ THIS KITCHEN DRAWER was mounted on full-extension drawer slides, so reaching all the plastic containers of essential supplies is easy and allows the drawer to function as a family command center.

Creating a Command Center

Whether you're married or single, live in small or large space, every household requires a specific place for handling all the paper and information related to daily life—things like schedules for school activities, invitations to parties, reminders for doctors' appointments, bills, and other necessary notices. And according to organizing experts, the best place for this command center is near an exterior door that everyone in the family must enter or exit at some point during the day. The easiest solution: a wall-mounted bulletin board with pockets for mail, messages, and writing supplies. Of course the center need not be the first thing you see when you walk in the door. For example, if you opt to use the front hall, consider hanging a notice board and a large envelope, basket, or folder for each family member on the back of a closet door or inside an armoire. While the message center will be out of sight to visiting guests, it won't be out of mind to family members who will have to go into the closet to put away outdoor gear.

▶ TO MAKE SURE YOUR FAMILY sees important notices, place your message center in close proximity to where they hang their coats when they come in the door. These cubbies were designed with a bulletin board on one end to accommodate invitations, shopping lists and other important notes.

Kitchens

In most homes, the kitchen is the hub—the one room where friends and family gather regularly to prepare meals, exchange stories, and catch up on the day's events. So why not make it an efficient workspace and an inviting place to hang out? Don't feel limited by the existing storage. And don't feel as though you need to do a full-blown remodel to make the space more functional. With a little ingenuity and a few store-bought accessories, you can efficiently tackle the pile of plates in your cupboards and the stacks of cookbooks that line your counters. You can deal with all of the plastic containers you've collected but never used, and finally make sense of that junk drawer. With a little forethought, pots and pans can be consolidated on a single rack near the stove, and linens and utensils can be corralled in baskets that are kept near the kitchen table. The goal is to arrange everything in a commonsense fashion so the heart of your home is both an easy place to use and an enjoyable place to gather.

◄ THE POTS IN THIS KITCHEN are contained on a rod that's recessed inside the framework of the cabinetry that surrounds the range. A plate rail is used to organize lids on the wall behind the pots, while cooking utensils are conveniently hung beneath the range hood.

Essential Ingredients

BECAUSE FOOD PREPARATION is a kitchen's primary purpose, there should be plenty of places for storing nonperishable items. How and where you do this depends both on how your kitchen is arranged and the quantity of supplies that you want to keep on hand. For example, if you shop once a month and buy in bulk, you'll probably find a walk-in pantry with generous shelf space most useful. If you shop at least once a week, however, you may be able to get by with several shelves in a single cabinet. In either case, the key to storing ingredients is having every item in view and within reach.

▲ TO MAKE IT EASIER to keep tabs on how much sugar, spice, or other dry goods remain in your pantry, remove these items from their packaging and store them in glass jars. Lining the jars on open shelves makes finding what you need a snap—especially when you're in a hurry.

◄ IF YOUR KITCHEN HAS AN ISLAND, make sure you're using it to it's best potential. Relegate cooking or serving gear there, to better the flow around the appliances.

◀ IF YOU BUY IN BULK and have run out of places to stash your savings, convert a closet near your kitchen into a small walk-in pantry. Install adjustable shelves and add a notice board to the back of the door so you can note when supplies are running low.

▲ LOCATED BELOW THE MICROWAVE, this extra-deep base cabinet is outfitted with pullout pantry shelves and stocked with snacks. Because it's outside the kitchen's main cooking zone, kids can grab items for after-school snacks without getting in the way of dinner preparations.

QUICK FIX

Counter Cures

Clear the clutter on kitchen countertops in five simple steps.

- Stash take-out menus in an expandable file folder. Sort the menus by cuisine, and place the file in a cabinet or drawer near the phone.
- If reading the paper is part of your morning ritual, place a basket near the breakfast table and toss the paper in it when you are done. Recycle when the basket is full.
- Transfer flour, sugar, rice, and other staples from bags to large, clear canisters or jars with airtight lids. Store those you use daily on your counter, and place the remainder in your pantry.
- Group whisks, spatulas, ladles, and other cooking utensils in vases, pitchers, or canisters.
- Dump your big, bulky appliances in favor of smaller versions that can easily mount underneath overhead cabinets.

FOODSTUFFS

▲ SO THAT YOU DON'T HAVE TO HUNT all over your kitchen for essential ingredients every time you want to bake a batch of cookies, keep all of your non-perishable supplies in one central place, like a large pantry cabinet with multiple layers of shelves.

▲ IF KITCHEN SPACE IS AT A PREMIUM, install a shelf about 12 in. from the ceiling. Use it to store items like rice and pasta that you don't need every-day. So you're able to see what's on hand without climbing a ladder, keep items in glass jars.

▲ BY ADDING RESTAURANT-GRADE metal shelves on either side of this freestanding range, the owners of this kitchen made it possible to keep cookbooks and cooking gear where they're needed. Topping the shelves with butcher block, which can function as a cutting board, adds to their usefulness.

◄ CONSIDER STORING STAPLES like flour, rice, and coffee in a base cabinet with glide-out drawers. Because the shelves pull toward you, you'll have an easy time finding what you need, even if it's stowed way in the back. Drawers with high sides ensure that items stay securely in place as the unit glides back and forth.

▼ IF YOU'RE SHORT ON STORAGE, think outside the box. Additional "pantry" space was added to this kitchen by lining one wall of the adjoining service staircase with floor-to-ceiling shelves that are deep enough to hold one bottle, can, or jar. Added bonus: This type of storage is also ideal for displaying decorative items like plates and platters.

▲ AN ODD ALCOVE left over from an earlier remodeling becomes a useful walk-in pantry in this kitchen. When organizing a space such as this, remember that shelving doesn't have to stop at your height; it can go all the way up to the ceiling and be used for stashing items that are reserved for special occasions.

◀ WHETHER YOU CHOOSE built-in or freestanding cabinets, outfitting an otherwise unused wall in a kitchen with floor-to-ceiling storage is always a wise investment since you can never have too many places to put things.

▼ TO FREE COUNTER SPACE for small appliances that you use on a regular basis, mount a shallow shelf in the open space between the bottom of the cupboard and the top of the counter. Use the shelf to store jars of baking ingredients, canisters, and other items that would otherwise clutter the counter.

Wine Storage Made Simple

It's fine to store everyday wine in the kitchen, but if you have an extensive collection—or exceptional bottles—a cool (50°F to 60°F), dry place, like a basement, is essential. And because wine should be stored on its side to prevent the cork from drying out and the wine from spoiling, you'll need bins or racks with angled shelves to hold the bottles in place. If a full-fledged wine cellar isn't an option, consider a wine refrigerator. Available in sizes that hold anywhere from 24 to more than 100 bottles, these specialized cooling centers can be installed under counters or islands or in a run of cabinets, just like a standard refrigerator or freezer.

▶ INSTALL WINE RACK DRAWER SLIDES to an existing base cabinet to make wine storage—and retrieval—simple.

SPICES

◀ THE EASIEST WAY to organize spices is by type of cuisine. Simply create a tray (an aluminum baking dish will work well) for Mexican or Indian dishes, for example, and fill several small containers with the essential spices. Label the tray as well as the individual containers so anyone can easily find what they need.

▲ THIS NARROW PULLOUT, which can be accessed from both sides, puts spices within close proximity to the cooktop, the area where they're used most. To cut down on prep time, store spices with those used most often on the top rack.

◀ FOR A LARGE COLLECTION OF SPICES, utilize a cabinet that can do double duty with a rack on the inside and one that's mounted on the back of the door. Place spices that are used every day on the door rack so they'll be in full view when you open the cabinet.

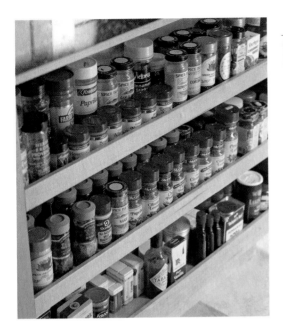

THE PROS KNOW

Store herbs and spices away from heat and light to preserve freshness and flavor. Replace them after six months because most herbs, by that time, have lost their potency.

◄ SMALL SHELVES WITH LIPS make organizing and identifying spices easy since the lips hold the bottles in place and you can easily see the label on each jar. Arrange the containers alphabetically to quickly find the spice your recipe calls for.

▲ CLUTTER ON THE COUNTERTOP is kept to a minimum in this sleek kitchen, where the spice rack is suspended over the cooktop from a stainless-steel rod. While this placement is fine for small amounts of frequently used spices, bulk storage should be located elsewhere, preferably in a cool, dry place.

Cooking Tools

GOOD FOOD CAN BE MADE FAST. The secret: efficient storage that puts all of your tools at your fingertips. The most obvious examples are metal racks for hanging pots and pans near a stove or cooktop. Other ideas include cabinets outfitted with vertical dividers to keep cookie sheets, cake pans, and baking items in good order, and canisters used to keep spoons, spatulas, and other utensils within easy reach. Even hanging a magnetic strip near your prep area for organizing knives will make slicing and dicing an effortless task. All of these ideas are simply starting points, however. By organizing the interiors of your cabinets, drawers, and pantry to suit your cooking style, you soon will have a kitchen that runs like a well-oiled machine.

▲ A POT RACK DOESN'T HAVE TO BE made of metal. It can also be crafted from wood, like this one, in a design that mimics your cabinets. The shelf above accommodates lids and pots that are too large to hang.

▲ MAKE A DEEP DRAWER more useful by organizing it with your collection of baking sheets and muffin trays stored vertically rather than horizontally in a stack. This will make it easier to find what you need.

▲ UNLESS YOU HAVE THE RIGHT ARRANGEMENT, storing pots and pans in cabinets can be a chore. Here, sliding bins keep cookware contained while offering simple access. To make it easy to find what you need, sort items by use. For example, keep your baking pans in one bin and your pots in another.

▲ POT RACKS ARE A PERFECT SOLUTION for serious cooks because they place cookware where it can be easily reached. To keep racks from becoming a jumbled mess, sort pots and pans by size, hanging the smallest in front and the largest in back.

The Inside Story on Storage

If your kitchen cabinets are bursting at the seams, sort through the contents and toss items you no longer need. Disposing of mismatched glasses, stacks of plastic containers, and broken appliances will free up valuable space and so will the following tasks:

- **Create deep storage.** Stash items that are used infrequently (think bread machines, food processors, and good china) on shelves in the garage, basement, or attic. Tape a running list of their locations inside one of your cabinets so you know where to find them when necessary.

- **Annex a wall.** Mount a sheet of pegboard or a metal rack on a wall near the range. Then, using hooks, hang your pots and pans.

- **Maximize shelf space.** Install hooks for hanging mugs and teacups. Add a wire rack to break up dishes into more manageable stacks.

- **Divide and conquer.** Retrofit a cabinet with a store-bought vertical racking system. Use it to keep unwieldy items like platters, baking sheets, and serving trays in order.

- **Retrofit existing cabinets.** Replace the shelves in base cabinets with full-extension pullout racks. This will make it easier to access formerly out-of-reach items.

POTS AND PANS

▲ TO KEEP YOUR DRAWER of plastic storage containers in good order, store them with lids intact. While this takes up a little more space, it saves time from hunting through a jumbled mess of mismatched tops and bottoms.

▼ KEEP ALL OF YOUR BAKING EQUIPMENT in one cupboard. To prevent the collection of trays, racks, and muffin tins from becoming a jumbled mess, outfit the cabinet with vertical dividers that will hold the pans upright.

▲ NO MATTER HOW LARGE YOUR KITCHEN, storing roasters and other oversized pans can be difficult especially since they rarely fit in standard size cabinets. Here, in this rustic kitchen, the pans are kept on a ceiling-mounted shelf out of the way, but within close reach.

THE PROS KNOW

The best way to ensure that your kitchen operates efficiently is to store items close to where you'll be using them. For example, hang pots and pans on a rack near the stove. Stash knives and cutting boards in a drawer near a prep sink. Store dinnerware close to the table or in close proximity to the dishwasher so cleanup is less of a chore.

Handy Uses for Hooks

- Hang dish towels to dry on the side of an island.
- Mount a rolling pin on a wall over a baking center.
- Attach pots and pans to a rack near the cooktop.
- Store mugs near the coffee maker.
- Hold wire baskets for keeping small items, like garlic and lemons, at the ready.

◀ WITH THE ADDITION of a wire grid, a common item at most home centers, an empty wall becomes easy-to-reach storage for pots, pans, and other cooking gear. Metal hooks hold the items in place.

▲ THE SMARTEST WAY TO ORGANIZE your kitchen is to place things at their point of use. Here, pots and pans are stored over the stove on hooks that attach to a metal rod, while cookbooks are kept on shelves beneath the island's prep surface.

COOKBOOKS

▲ IF YOU PREFER a clutter-free kitchen but your cookbook collection is extensive, consider stowing the volumes out of sight in deep drawers designed to hold pots or in cabinets with slide-out shelves. These custom cabinets slide out from the wall.

▲ KEEP ALL OF YOUR RECIPES in one place by storing cookbooks together on a dedicated set of shelves. When determining where to place them in your kitchen, look for a space that's within close proximity to the stove but also adjacent to ample counter space so there's room to spread out and work.

▲ STORING COOKBOOKS ON SHELVES that are part of a centrally located kitchen island makes them easily accessible from all points in the kitchen. Arranging the books by cuisine makes it easy to find a particular recipe.

▲ TO HELP CREATE a display shelf for cookbooks, the homeowners simply removed the doors from a set of cabinets, creating a cookbook niche.

▶ BY INCORPORATING SHELVING FOR COOKBOOKS above this desk, a kitchen niche becomes a dedicated space for planning family dinners. If you have a similar spot in your kitchen but cabinet doors cover the shelves, remove the doors to make it easier to access your family's favorite recipes.

THE PROS KNOW

Place recipes clipped from newspapers and magazines in plastic sleeves, and then store the sleeves in a three-ring binder. To help make finding a recipe easier, sort them by cuisine, occasion, prep time, or some other significant designator.

Dishware

A WELL-ORGANIZED KITCHEN will make cooking less of a chore; it will also simplify the serving process. To put your dishes, utensils, and linens in order, start by taking inventory of what you own, dividing the items into groupings based on how they are used. Everyday dinnerware is best kept on open shelves or in cabinets that are in close proximity to where you eat breakfast, lunch, and dinner. Seldom-used items, like Grandma's holiday china, are better stored in a secure location away from the bustling workspace such as the basement or attic. Padded containers will protect fine dinnerware from dust and damage.

▼ IF YOUR EVERYDAY DISHES don't stay organized behind closed doors, then try this stylish yet practical makeover: Store them in open shelves so that you know exactly where to turn when you need a specific item. If you have more than one set of dishes, stow plates, bowls, and cups according to color and size.

▲ CABINETS WITH BUILT-IN DISH DIVIDERS make it easy to retrieve dinnerware without pulling out an entire stack of dishes.

▼ DO YOU PREFER TO STORE your china behind closed doors? Then consider cabinets with shallow pullout shelves for convenient access. To make it easy to find what you need, store only like items on a shelf. For example, organize all of your covered serving dishes in one area and serving bowls in another.

▲ WIRE SHELVES ARE A SIMPLE SOLUTION for small budgets. What's more, they're easy to install and can be mounted anywhere—even over the range or cooktop, where they can be used to warm plates before serving.

Shelving Solutions

Increase the storage capacity of cabinets with the following store-bought accessories:

- Plate racks. Those with vertical slots prevent plates from rubbing against one another and chipping.
- Shelf maximizers. These wire racks with legs add a second layer to an ordinary shelf, allowing you to condense dishware into a smaller space by stacking cups and saucers over plates and bowls.
- Pullouts. Because these wire or plastic baskets slide out, you'll be able to reach items in the back with ease.
- Tiered racks. These stair-stepped shelves let you see with ease everything you've stored.
- Cabinet door racks. These devices convert the inside of cabinet doors into convenient storage spaces for foils and plastic wraps, even pot lids.

▼ DON'T WORRY if your cabinets can't accommodate oversized bowls, baskets, and serving platters. Take a cue from this kitchen by stacking them on an open baker's rack or even on a bookshelf.

▲ A WALL-MOUNTED DRYING RACK adds vintage charm to this classic kitchen while serving as a storage spot for dinnerware. Because the rack is mounted directly over the sink where dishes are washed, it makes cleanup easy. To glean extra storage for cleaning supplies, the homeowner curtained the area below the sink.

◄ BECAUSE THE OWNERS OF THIS KITCHEN eat most of their meals at the room's central island, they opted for a design with open shelving on one side so everyday dinnerware is kept close at hand. Added bonus: Because the shelves are shallow, things aren't likely to end up lost in the back.

▲ THERE'S NO REASON WHY your dishes should be hidden away in cabinets. Instead, use them to enhance your room's décor. Here, pastel-colored china adds a splash of color to this all-white kitchen.

Storage for Safekeeping

Here's how to store fine flat-ware, china, and linens so that they're ready to use when you need them.

- Keep silver and silver-plated flat-ware in trays lined with velvet, felt, or another soft fabric to prevent scratches.
- Store platters, candlesticks, and other large silver pieces in fabric bags. If you place more than one item in a bag, place a piece of felt between each one.
- Set wine glasses and other delicate crystal mouth up to avoid damage.
- Place good china and glassware in quilted containers to protect pieces from dust and help prevent chipping and cracking.
- Reduce wrinkles by rolling fine linens in acid-free tissue around a cardboard tube. Store the tube in a drawer until needed.

▲ TO CONVERT THIS KITCHEN CLOSET into stylish storage, the owners replaced its standard wood doors with a more charming French pair and added wood paneling to the interior walls. The closet's extra-deep shelves afford plenty of room for keeping everyday dishes up front where they're easy to reach and seldom-used items in the back.

▼ THE CEILING-MOUNTED SHELF over this kitchen countertop is open on both sides so that dishes can be readily accessed from the dining and serving areas. Dividing the shelf into several smaller compartments simplifies the process of sorting glasses, cups, plates, and bowls.

▼ IF YOU HAVE AN EXTENSIVE COLLECTION of dinnerware, borrow an idea from the past—group your dishes by pattern, then stow them in glass-fronted cabinets. The glass doors serve a dual purpose: They make it simple to locate a particular design, and they keep the dishes dust free.

▲ ERGONOMIC ALTERNATIVES to traditional cabinets, drawers keep dishes at waist level, eliminating heavy overhead lifting. Wooden pegs, which can easily be reconfigured depending on what's stored, prevent dishes from sliding when the drawer is opened or closed.

▲ OPEN STORAGE allows for quick and easy access to dishes at a moment's notice. But it looks messy if not kept in some sense of order. Although it's ideal to keep like items together, you can mix things up provided the items share a common thread, like color or theme.

◄ IF YOU LACK DRAWER SPACE or want easy access to utensils while cooking, use simple ceramic or glass jars to keep wooden spoons, forks, and spatulas organized on your counter.

▼ RATHER THAN STOW EVERYDAY LINENS in drawers, which can be difficult to close when they're too full, stack them in baskets. The slide-out variety shown here is only available with cabinets made specifically for them, but you can create a similar scenario by simply stacking baskets on open shelves.

▲ SHALLOW DRAWERS with fitted dividers are essential for sorting silverware. Thanks to a double-tray design, this drawer can accommodate two sets. Although custom dividers are ideal, alternatives, such as wire or plastic containers, can be found at most home stores.

◄ WHILE DRAWER DIVIDERS ARE ESSENTIAL for sorting cutlery, those that can be removed make setting the table a snap since they allow knives, forks, and spoons to be carried to the table with ease.

Clean Sweep

What's the secret to a clean kitchen? Turns out it's keeping the area surrounding the sink clean. Here are a few ideas for keeping this often busy area tidy:

- Annex empty space, like the area immediately under the front of your sink. Install a narrow tilt-out drawer, and use it to hide sponges, scrub brushes, and scouring pads.
- Group garbage and recycling containers on a slide-out rack beneath the sink or island. Place several garbage bags in the bottom of each can so a new bag will be ready when a full one is removed.
- Store cleaning solutions and dishwashing detergents in pullout baskets or bins under the sink.
- If space permits, add a plate rack over the sink. Dishes are easiest to handle if stored between waist and chest height near where they are cleaned.

▲ A CENTRALLY LOCATED SET of recycling bins makes cleanup simple. For easier access, mount the containers on glide-out racks and conceal them behind cabinet doors.

◀ OUTFITTED WITH A GALVANIZED METAL TRAY, this tilt-out drawer, which can be retrofitted to existing cabinetry, turns what would otherwise be wasted space into a handy place for stashing sponges and scouring brushes. When closed, the tray's façade matches the style of the surrounding cabinets.

Gathering Places

Aside from your kitchen, what's the one room in your house that receives heavy use on a daily basis? More than likely it's the den or the living room—the space that holds the TV and all of your other media equipment, books, toys, and games. And whether this room is furnished formally with fine upholstered furniture or is more casual with a pair of slipcovered sofas, chances are it collects clutter. Why? Because trying to find places to stow all the stuff that make this room a great place to hang out in can be a challenge.

In addition to the usual media equipment (TV, DVD player, and stereo), there are bound to be stacks of books and magazines. If you have children, there will inevitably be a pile of toys. The solution to creating order in this space isn't to do away with the various pieces of equipment and things that entertain us, but rather to find ways of making them disappear when they're not in use. A wall of simple store-bought shelves, for example, can help you convert stacks of reading material into a well-organized library. A more costly but stream-lined solution is to install built-in cabinets, which in addition to containing books can also be used to conceal media equipment behind closed doors. The bottom line to organizing this active room is to keep items out of sight but not out of mind.

◀ WHEN PLANNING A WALL OF BUILT-INS, think about how they'll fit in with the overall design of your space. Here, tall, narrow cases were selected to complement the striped paint treatment used on the walls. Several drawers below a built-in bench provide extra storage.

Media Equipment

I N THE PAST, MOST LIVING ROOMS WERE DESIGNED so that the fireplace was the focal point of the space. Today, however, the fireplace has been replaced by the TV—a move that many decorators lament for the simple reason that a TV surrounded by all of its accompanying equipment (DVD player, speakers, and cable box) is anything but an attractive site. Built-ins, cubbies, or storage units can easily correct the problem, but the proper placement is essential. After all, you want the screen to be visible from any angle but positioned so that glare won't interfere with daytime viewing. You'll also want to make sure that the storage device you choose, be it an armoire or set of shelves, can accommodate media accessories such as DVDs, CDs, and videos. Finally, get a handle on all of your components' cords and cables by utilizing ties or flexible tubing devices. Doing so will eliminate a tangled mess of wires and create a truly well-organized—and visually appealing—media center.

▲ A TALL AND NARROW CLOSET is transformed into a multilevel media center with the simple addition of custom shelves. Before retrofitting a closet or recessed space, look for electrical outlets. If none exist, have an electrician install one prior to construction.

Custom built-ins may be a good way to create unobtrusive storage for large items like televisions and stereos, but don't overlook the rest of the room. It also helps to buy furniture that can do double duty—coffee tables with drawers and end tables with shelves—by providing auxiliary places to tuck things, like the TV remote or a pad of paper for jotting notes, that are used everyday.

▼ IF YOU WANT TO CONCEAL MEDIA EQUIPMENT but can't justify the expense of custom built-ins or a large armoire, borrow this clever idea by stacking your equipment on a sturdy set of unfinished shelves. Disguise the unit by covering the frame with standard tab-top curtain panels.

▲ MEDIA EQUIPMENT doesn't have to be kept in an armoire. Here, a set of three niches, the largest sized to hold a television, convert an empty wall into a contemporary media cabinet. When adopting a design solution such as this, be sure to have electrical outlets installed at the back of each niche.

◄ TODAY'S LARGE-SCREEN TVS can easily overwhelm a room— even one like this with generous proportions. To prevent that from happening, try to visually minimize its impact on the space, such as recessing it into the wall cavity as was done here. This also allowed space for shelves above it, for storing other media equipment.

Streamline Media Equipment

Organize your media equipment in a snap by following these five easy steps:

- Group all of your equipment in a single cabinet or built-in.
- Invest in a universal remote that will control all of your equipment.
- Recess speakers into walls and ceilings where they don't take up valuable floor or shelf space.
- Transfer old cassette and video tapes you wish to keep to narrower space-saving CDs or DVDs. Throw out the old cassettes and tapes.
- Eliminate unused components. For example, if you haven't taken your turntable for a spin in years, it's time to get rid of it.

▼ A GEOMETRIC-SHAPED RECESS with custom shelving and cabinetry turns what would otherwise have been a blank wall into a full-fledged media center. Slide-out wire bins to the left of the television provide plenty of easy-access storage for DVDs.

◄ IN THIS MODERN LIVING ROOM, all eyes are focused on the TV, a flat-screen style that's incorporated into a custom-made built-in. The surrounding shelves provide ample storage space for books as well as for displaying decorative items. Below, drawers and cabinets conceal additional media and electronic equipment.

► THE OWNERS OF THIS MUSIC COLLECTION chose to stash their CDs in cabinets fitted with shallow slide-out shelves—a storage solution that makes it simple to search for a particular CD since cases are kept on end with the album title clearly visible.

Caring for Electrical Cords

Finding a place to put your media equipment is easy. Deciding how to handle the cords and wires that accompany the television, cable box, stereo receiver, and other components can be slightly more complicated, especially if your electrical outlets aren't in an accessible location. Fortunately, there are a number of easy-to-implement solutions available, like Velcro® ties, plastic clips, flexible tubing, and labels, many of which can be found at your local hardware store or home center.

◄ BECAUSE MEDIA CENTERS ARE COMPRISED of two or more pieces of equipment, electrical cords often become tangled and difficult to manage. Flexible plastic tubing, available at home centers, allow you to gather and conceal several cords, streamlining the surrounding area in the process.

► WHEN MORE THAN ONE CORD plugs into a power strip, it can be difficult to determine which cord belongs to what component. To solve that problem, identify each piece of equipment on a file folder label and then wrap it around each cord.

◄ A STRATEGICALLY PLACED POWER STRIP can prevent overload at a wall outlet by eliminating the need for long extension cords. To keep the cord that connects the strip to your power outlet from becoming tangled, first wind it in an oval pattern, and cinch its middle with a Velcro band or twist-ties from loaves of bread.

▶ WHEN ORGANIZING CDS AND DVDS, borrow an idea from a library. Stow the media devices in shallow drawers and outfit the drawer fronts with handles that accommodate labels. This way you'll be able to see at a glance where things are kept.

▲ STORAGE UNITS SIZED TO THEIR CONTENTS help keep the items organized and can maximize the space. This cabinet does double duty, with the CD storage unit inset into the cabinet, allowing enough room for a door-mounted cassette holder.

▲ JUST BECAUSE YOUR DVDS AND DVD player are hidden behind a cabinet door doesn't mean they shouldn't be organized. Divide the cabinet into sections, with each sized to house a specific component of your entertainment system. Shallow drawers should also be added to accommodate CDs and DVDs.

Remote Solutions

Whether you operate your TV with one remote control and your DVD player with another or have one complex unit that controls all of your media and audio equipment, establishing a dedicated storage space for your components' remotes will save you from having to look under the couch and turn over seat cushions every time you want a little entertainment. Here are a few creative places to store your family's most coveted item:

• Hand-sewn pouches that overlap a chair or sofa arm.
• A lidded decorative box on a coffee or side table.
• A small leather tray that can rest on a table next to your favorite chair.
• Small basket or bottle caddies with handles.

▲ BOTH PRINT AND ELECTRONIC MEDIA can happily coexist. The secret: designing a set of shelves that can accommodate both. To do so, you'll need to know the measurements of both your television and your books. You'll also need to have the shelving unit designed to accommodate an electrical connection.

Books

OOKS, UNLIKE MANY OF THE BELONGINGS that clutter our homes, have the ability to add warmth and personality to any room. To have the most impact, however, your personal reading material should be grouped as a collection in one space. To that end, begin by taking inventory of your library, noting not only the subject matter (fiction, gardening, and history, for example) but also the dimensions of the books in your possession. Taking inventory at the start will help you determine the type as well as the dimensions of the shelving system you require. If your collection is small and comprised only of a few paperback novels, for instance, a simple store-bought bookcase will most likely meet your needs. If, however, you're an avid reader with an extensive library covering multiple topics, you may want to invest in something more substantial, like a wall of built-ins that not only houses your collection but also shows it off.

▶ IF YOUR BUDGET CAN'T ACCOMMODATE BUILT-INS, take a cue from this room and devise a basic shelving system that fits the look of the space. Here, to complement the room's clean, modern design, the owners of this space devised a shelving system using simple pine planks artfully arranged in a grid pattern.

▼ ALTHOUGH FLOOR-TO-CEILING BOOKSHELVES are a nice feature, sometimes they can make a spare, modern space feel cluttered. One way to prevent that from happening is to install a pair of sliding doors in front of the shelves. Then, when not in use, the bookshelves simply disappear.

▲ INSTEAD OF SIMPLY stacking books on an ottoman or coffee table, place them in tray. Not only is the presentation neater, but the books are also less likely to wind up on the floor.

THE PROS KNOW

To make finding specific book titles easier, organize your library by subject, using bookends or other sturdy decorative objects to denote where one section ends and another begins. If your collection is sizeable and requires additional shelving space, remove cookbooks and store them on a shelf or in a cabinet in the kitchen.

▲ WHEN ADDING BOOKCASES to a room, don't necessarily go for the wall with the most open surface area. Instead, look for smaller spaces that would otherwise be left unused. Here, they were added to a half wall that hides a staircase, further delineating the separation of space.

THE PROS KNOW

▶ THE BEAUTY OF BOOKCASES is that they can go just about anywhere. Here, thanks to the addition of simple open shelving, an otherwise useless alcove becomes a cozy reading nook.

▼ INSTEAD OF LINING AN EMPTY WALL with floor-to-ceiling shelves, the owners of this space chose to place their units on either side of a doorway. The resulting symmetry not only makes for a more interesting entrance, but it also creates balance in the space.

Designing Shelves

While it's important that a bookcase fit the dimensions of the room in which you place it, it's equally important that it accommodate your collection of books. Here's how to find a set of shelves that will do both:

- To determine the number of shelves you need, measure the linear footage of the books, CDs, and other items you intend to store. For example, a shelf measuring 6 ft. in length offers 6 lin. ft. of storage.
- Measure the area of the room where the shelves will go.
- When commissioning a custom bookshelf, request that the depth of the shelf be 12 in. This will allow you to store most any size book with ease.
- Consider the weight of your collection. To ensure adequate support, shelves should be constructed out of wood that is no less than $3/4$ in. thick.
- For added support, place shelf supports every 30 in. If this is not possible because of space limits, restrict shelf length to no more than 30 in.
- Always leave room for extra shelves so your collection can expand.

▲ WITH FLOOR SPACE FILLED TO CAPACITY, the owners of this modern apartment took advantage of the double-height ceiling, using the extra wall space to install shelving units for books and display items around the perimeter of the room.

▶ STORAGE, ESPECIALLY FOR THINGS LIKE BOOKS, doesn't have to be confined to an actual room. Here, built-in shelving is used to give a hallway leading into a living room a second purpose.

Book Basics

I f you want to make books last, dust them periodically using a vacuum with a brush attachment. Here are a few other important tips for maintaining your collection:

- Loosely pack hardcover books on shelves—with large books stored flat to avoid bending their spines—and arrange according to subject. Use bookends for even support, and leave dust jackets in place to protect covers.
- Line up small paperbacks vertically. Stack oversized paperbacks to avoid warping their spines.
- Keep books with leather covers at moderate temperature and humidity levels. Heat and dryness can crack tanned leather, and dampness can cause swelling.

▲ STANDARD SIZE BOOKCASES are great, but for a truly custom fit you need a built-in, like this unit, which acts as both book storage and room divider. It provides the perfect backdrop for the sofa, and allows for easy removal and storage of books.

▲ IF YOUR READING COLLECTION is small and space is at a premium, consider a coffee table with shelves that can accommodate several stacks of books.

◄ THIS SPACE IS WELL ORGANIZED and tidy even though it's filled with lots of furniture. The sofa table acts as a backup to the bookshelf for book storage.

▲ THE CUSTOMIZED SHELVING in this living room is shallow but holds quite a few books and accessories due to the use of adjustable shelves, which allow for maximum flexibility.

Private Spaces

Let's face it: Life is complicated, and it's not always possible to leave the pressures of the world around us outside the home. That's why within every home there needs to be an escape—a private place where we can relax and unwind when the day is done. In most homes, this responsibility falls on the master suite, the one area of the house that's already off limits to everyone but immediate family. But relaxing, even in rooms that are designed specifically for this purpose, can be difficult, especially when the floor is covered with clothes that haven't been put away or the bathroom counter is clogged with so many toiletries that it looks like a shelf at your local drugstore. The solution: Find a convenient place for everything by purging your belongings and reworking or adding to your existing storage. Start small. Clean off a shelf in your linen closet so there's a place to store excess grooming products. Then assess your furnishings. Would replacing a small bedside table with a chest of drawers help your organizing issues? Finally, take an inventory of your wardrobe. If you haven't worn an item in more than a year, get rid of it and free up some valuable closet space. After all, less really is more.

◄ **WHEN IT COMES TO MAXIMIZING STORAGE** in the bedroom, don't overlook the space under the bed or surrounding it. Just as nightstands work wonders for keeping reading materials close at hand, a chest at the foot of the bed provides easy-access storage for spare blankets and pillows.

Bedrooms

EDROOMS, NO MATTER THEIR SIZE, never seem to have enough storage. As a result, clothes pile up at the foot of the bed and the night table becomes buried in a stack of books. The result is a retreat that's anything but restful. To remedy the situation, take stock of what you store in the space. For example, do you really need those plaid pants you haven't worn in five years? Once you weed out the things that are no longer necessary, you'll find that it's much easier to organize the room. If, for instance, you are an avid reader, you may want to consider a headboard that incorporates shelving. If the culprit is an excess of clothing, you may to need to invest in a larger chest of drawers or a set of shallow storage boxes that can slide neatly under your bed. What you'll discover as you assess the contents of the room is that with a little planning it's quite possible to create a space where everything has its place.

▲ LOOKING FOR AN EASY WAY to keep clothes from piling up on the bedroom floor? Install racks of pegs or hooks around the perimeter of your room. You'll find them useful for holding everything from bathrobes and belts to purses and pants.

◀ ONE OF THE BENEFITS OF BUILT-INS is that they can make an otherwise useless space, like the area between the bed and a wall, useful. The unit here, a sort of sideboard that butts up to the edge of the bed, features shelves that are deep enough to accommodate various night-table necessities.

THE PROS KNOW

When space is tight, purchase low-profile storage boxes and bins. Fill them with out-of-season clothing and stash the items under the bed.

▲ IF YOU'RE AN AVID NIGHTTIME READER but your bedside table is too small to cope with a large stack of books, add a set of recessed shelves over the bed. If you don't feel like knocking into a wall or if built-ins aren't in your budget, opt for a simple store-bought unit.

Create a Restful Retreat

Here's how to make sure that clutter isn't the last thing you see when you go to bed at night or the first thing you see when you wake up in the morning.

- Outfit the top drawer in your dresser or bedside table with small plastic containers, shallow boxes, or baskets in which to store bedroom supplies and accessories like watches and rings.
- Fit the backs of closet doors with hooks that can be used to hold accessories that tend to pile up on chairs and benches.
- Move your current reading material off your nightstand, and store it on a nearby shelf or in a basket under the bed.

▲ THIS SLEEPING SPOT OWES its spare appearance to a wall of built-in cupboards opposite the foot of the bed. To keep the drawers from becoming a mess, identify one for each type of clothing, like socks and undergarments, shirts, sweaters, and anything else that needs to be folded.

THE PROS KNOW

To prevent dirty clothes from piling up on the bedroom floor, outfit your closet with hampers or laundry bags for colored, white, and dry-clean-only wash. Then, when you get undressed, place what you've worn in the appropriate bag and your clothes will be ready for the laundry.

▼ SOMETIMES THE SIMPLEST IDEAS are the best. Here, a recessed shelf replaces the headboard, providing a place to stash reading materials, glasses, and a host of other necessities that may be needed in the middle of the night.

The Nature of Nightstands

When it comes to choosing bedside storage, forgo the expected matching nightstands in favor of a mixed set that fits your needs as well as your partner's. Here's what to consider:

- Bedside tables that include shelves are ideal for those who not only like to read in bed but also like to keep a stack of books on hand at all times.

- A chest of drawers is a wise choice if you have supplies for a hobby, such as knitting, that you like to work on in bed before retiring for the night.

- Some pieces of furniture can perform more than one function. When not holding a stack of books, a sturdy hall chair can provide a comfortable place to sit while putting on shoes.

- A small, round table fits the bill if you have nothing to stash, save for an alarm clock and a lamp.

▲ THE ADJUSTABLE SHELVES that frame the window in this guest bedroom turn otherwise wasted space into practical storage for books and other treasures. The daybed is another practical space saver because it can be used for an overnight guest or as a quiet place to read.

▼ INSTALL A NIGHTSTAND with drawers so that you can easily conceal books, magazines, knitting supplies, and other potential clutter from view.

▲ LOW-PROFILE BUILT-IN SHELVES on either side of this room's bed accomplish two goals. First, they provide ample storage for books and other necessities. Second, thanks to a slim profile and a paint color that matches the floor, they are hardly visible, adding to the spare look of the space.

Closets and Dressing Rooms

I F YOU'RE LUCKY, EVEN YOUR SMALLEST BEDROOM has a closet of some sort where you can keep your clothes. The problem is, most closets, whether a narrow reach-in or a generous walk-in, are ill-equipped to handle the wardrobes we expect to stuff in them. The result? Clothing ends up piled on the floor or on a bedside chair. But it doesn't have to be this way. You can make small changes that will yield big benefits. For example, a door-mounted rack can help get your shoes off the floor, and hanging sweater bags can give you additional shelf space without the hassle, or expense, of construction. With the right organizing solution, you can have a closet that will not only accommodate all of your clothing, shoes, and accessories but also will make it easier to put them away at night and find them again in the morning.

▲ THE SECRET TO TAMING UNRULY DRESSER DRAWERS: Outfit them with store-bought containers intended for office supplies. To determine the containers and quantity that you will need, sort your accessories into categories before heading to the store.

▲ CREATE A SEPARATE DRESSING AREA to prevent clothing from cluttering the bedroom. The space can be an entire room or a closet that is deep enough to walk into. If you don't have a walk-in space, purchase a rolling cart that fits inside your closet. When you need to get dressed, simply roll out the cart.

Clothing Measurements

B efore purchasing a premade storage system, ensure a perfect fit by checking the dimensions of the various components against these common clothing measurements:

- Hats: 11 in. wide
- Handbags: 9 in. high
- Shirts, sport coats, and skirts: 38 in. long
- Dresses: 65 in. long
- Folded pants: 30 in. long
- Shoes: 12 in. deep
- Boots: 18 in. high

Essential Closet Organizers

If your closet is out of control, the following organizing products found at hardware stores and home centers can help you restore order. What's more, each of these products attaches directly to the closet's rod, so installation is a snap.

- **Handbag file.** Eight clear plastic sleeves attached to a single hanger. Each sleeve can accommodate one large bag or several smaller clutch styles.
- **Pocket shoe bags.** Similar in design to a handbag file, except each pocket holds a pair of shoes.
- **Sweater bags.** Vertical shelves designed to hold stacks of folded sweaters or shirts.
- **Jewelry organizer.** Clear vinyl bags that contain anywhere from 30 to 80 small pockets for organizing earrings, pins, and other small accessories.

◀ CONVERT A SMALL BEDROOM into a walk-in closet by installing kitchen-style cabinets, which can be purchased for very little money at any home center. The glass-fronted doors used to create this space are attractive and practical, protecting the contents from dust, while allowing the owner to see easily what's stored inside.

An Organized Adult's Closet

These recommendations from the National Closet Group can be used as a guide in configuring an adult's closet.

- 12 in. to 14 in. between sweater shelves (shelf depth: 16 in.)
- 6 in. between shoe shelves (shelf depth: 12 in. to 14 in.)
- For double-hanging rods, place top rod 80 in. high, allowing two sections of about 40 in.
- Depth: 24 in. for suits and dresses; 28 in. for coats
- 55 in. for medium-length garments
- 63 in. for long garments
- Belt hook: 50 in. from floor
- 40 in. for suits, shirts, and skirts

▲ IF NEAT PILES AREN'T YOUR FORTE, outfit closet shelves with lined baskets or covered boxes. Attach labels, or a Polaroid picture in the case of shoes, so that it's easy to find what you're looking for.

▲ THIS CONTEMPORARY CLOSET ARRANGEMENT pairs drawers and shelves in one wall-mounted unit. To organize this type of set up, use the shelf space for things that are currently in season and the drawer below for things that are not. Simply switch items when the seasons change.

▶ EVEN STANDARD-SIZE CLOSETS can be made more functional by replacing the usual single shelf and rod with a store-bought system made of either wood or wire. Before making a purchase, take inventory of what you own so you are sure to buy the right components, like bins or boxes for odd-shaped items.

▲ READY-MADE CLOSET ACCESSORIES like hanging shoe bags and covered boxes, which can be found at most major retail stores, offer a less expensive alternative to a complete custom redo.

QUICK FIX

Closet Cleanup

Here's how to organize your closet in five simple steps:

1. Empty the closet of all its contents.
2. Vacuum and dust the interior.
3. Sort clothing by categories: jackets, pants, skirts, dresses, shirts, shoes, and so forth. Give to charity anything you have not worn in at least a year.
4. Pick a category and start returning items from that group to the closet. Sort items that you are returning by season and color.
5. Once everything is in place, use permanent markers so you'll always know where something goes. For example, add decorative labels to the front of each shelf to delineate what's to be stored.

Bathrooms

LARGE OR SMALL, SHARED OR PRIVATE, bathrooms have undergone significant changes over the last several years. Utilitarian spaces are out and spa-like retreats are in. But in the rush to create a comfortable place to relax after a hard day at work, don't overlook the obvious. Towels and toiletries still need a place to call home. So do supplies like toilet paper a nd cleaning gear. If you have the room, many of these things can be hidden from view in cabinets or other freestanding containers. If not, you might need to convert a nearby closet to an auxiliary storage space, or add a wall-mounted medicine cabinet or a set of shelves that can accommodate deep storage baskets. The end result will be a bath in which spending time is blissful.

▼ THE SECRET TO SUCCESSFUL STORAGE is always to keep items in close proximity to where they are needed. Here, a wall of cubbies provides easy access for towels and other bathing supplies. But open storage isn't for everyone. If you're not meticulous about how things are put away, the room's "clean" look can quickly disappear.

◀ A SIMPLE SOLUTION FOR ORGANIZING TOWELS in a shared family bath: Install a rail with pegs and designate a peg for each person. Avoid confusion by either labeling the pegs with each family member's name or assigning each person a different color towel.

◀ IF BUILT-INS AREN'T TO YOUR LIKING, borrow an idea from Victorian homes and furnish the bath with freestanding furniture. Here, a stainless-steel bench and towel rack keep toiletries and fresh towels within close proximity to the tub.

▲ PEDESTAL SINKS ARE PRETTY, but they don't provide much space for storing grooming supplies. One way to remedy the situation is to mount a shelf over the sink. The least obtrusive options are glass designs. Another idea: Utilize the molding that caps the wainscoting behind the sink as a secondary storage shelf.

Essential Bathroom Organizers

The following accessories found at hardware stores and home centers can help bring order to your bathroom:

- **Clear jars or canisters.** Fill them with cotton balls, swabs, and other small items.
- **Drawer and cabinet organizers.** These square and rectangular containers are ideal for grouping tubes of toothpaste, cosmetics, and other small toiletries.
- **Hooks.** Perhaps the most versatile storage device, these can be mounted anywhere and used to hold a basket filled with hand soaps or a pocket organizer for sorting toiletries.
- **Shower caddies.** Use them to organize your bathing essentials such as soap, shampoo, and sponges.
- **Stackable bins.** If your bath lacks cabinets, these bins, which can be stacked in a corner or placed beneath a pedestal sink, can provide storage space.

▲ SMALL BATHROOMS call for creativity. Here, dead wall space was converted to a narrow set of built-in shelves sized to accommodate both towels and toiletries.

THE PROS KNOW

If the space in your bath is limited, make every inch count by creating a "pocket" in the natural voids that fall between wall studs. Although narrow in depth, these spaces can be finished with drywall and tile and outfitted with shelves to accommodate toiletries, hand towels, and other small items.

▲ IN THIS BATH, LESS IS MORE. With only a simple storage shelf over each sink, the owners have to carefully select what toiletries to store. The result: a bath that's spare but serene.

▲ THIS BATHROOM OWES its orderly appearance to a variety of storage solutions that provide a place for everything. Open shelves beneath the sink house towels, while cleaning products are concealed in a closed cabinet. The niche to the left of the mirror provides a place for toiletries, helping to reduce counter clutter.

◄ NO LINEN CLOSET? NO PROBLEM. Here, a wall-mounted coat rack with an upper storage shelf works wonders. The hooks that would normally hold coats and hats can be used for robes and wet towels. The shelf can be used to store fresh linens or even toiletries or supplies.

▼ INSTEAD OF USING A DOOR to separate the toilet from the rest of the bath, the designer of this space created a custom wall that incorporates a rack for reading material as well as a shelf for supplies. If custom isn't an option, you can create a similar solution by using a narrow, freestanding bookshelf.

QUICK FIX

Clean Up the Medicine Cabinet

Organize your medicine cabinet in five simple steps.

1. Take everything out of the cabinet.
2. Discard any expired prescriptions or toiletries that you no longer use.
3. Remove any duplicate or surplus items, and store them in an alternate place, like a linen closet.
4. Divide what's left into categories such as medications, oral hygiene, first aid, and shaving equipment. Place cotton balls and swabs into small jars or canisters that fit inside the cabinet.
5. Return everything to the cabinet, keeping like items together. If space permits, designate a shelf for each category. If not, divide shelves using plastic bins, grouping the contents of one category in each bin.

▲ TWO MEDICINE CABINETS can be better than one—especially in a shared bath. Not only do they create a balanced display, but with a cabinet for each person, counters stay cleaner because there's more space to stow things.

▼ THE KEY TO KEEPING HARMONY in a shared space is to provide plenty of places for everyone's things. In this master bath, that meant installing two sinks with two mirrors separated by a narrow cabinet for storing soaps, toothpaste, and other shared supplies.

▲ WHEN THE TIME COMES TO FURNISH A BATH, think of the room as you would any other in your home. Instead of adding costly built-in cabinets, use furniture. A dresser with deep drawers can be used to keep both towels and toiletries tidy and out of sight.

▲ THE SHELF IN THIS TUB AREA offers a great opportunity to display decorative bottles and dishware. Put those pieces to practical use by filling them with soap and shampoo. More shelves or a towel rack on the unused wall could replace the chair if you need floor space.

◄ THIS BATH'S LADDER-STYLE STORAGE UNIT is in keeping with the room's clean appearance. The frameless mirror mounted over the sink conceals a deep storage cabinet, allowing for a contemporary counterless sink. And because the sink is wall mounted, there's plenty of extra space below for bins or a rolling cabinet should extra storage be required.

◀ IN THIS SMALL BATH, every bit of space is used to best advantage, from the wall-mounted towel bars to the bench and storage ledge around the bathtub.

▲ ALWAYS MOUNT HOOKS for hand towels near the sink so guests can easily find them. Place a basket below the sink to catch soiled cloths.

▲ MAKE YOUR LIFE EASY and put decorative surfaces to work. This large deck is a great place for towels. The handsome soap holder over the tub is as much decorative as it is practical.

Small Space Solutions

Maximize space in a powder room by using one of these inventive ideas:

- Keep only the supplies that you are presently using on hand. Place everything else in a closet outside the bathroom or on a shelf in the garage or basement.
- Install two standard-size towel bars or hooks on the back of the bathroom door for hanging towels and bathrobes.
- Utilize the area over the toilet for wall-mounted shelves. Make sure they are deep enough to accommodate standard-size toiletries.

- Outfit bathroom cabinets with stackable containers to corral toiletries and supplies. If the cabinet is deep enough, a door-mounted spice rack can accomplish the same purpose.
- Install a wall-mounted holder at the sink for toothbrushes and toothpaste. Add a hook for a hair dryer. In the shower, hang a storage caddy from the shower-head or install wall-mounted baskets or dispensers for soap and shampoo.

▲ THIS POWDER ROOM SHOWCASES a number of innovative ideas, like the wall-mounted wire basket used for towel storage. The deep molding installed around the perimeter of the space provides overflow storage for essential supplies.

6

Kids' Spaces

In any household where children are present, you're certain to find toys, books, and clothing strewn throughout most rooms. Short of banishing kids to their own wing, there's little you can do to stop these small messes from occurring. What you can do, however, is make it easier for them to round up their belongings by selecting a range of age-appropriate storage solutions. For example, if your children are elementary age or younger, provide rolling carts and baskets with handles that are easy for small hands to lift and tote to a designated spot. Once your child has graduated from building blocks and dolls to computer games and music, assign a shelf for their belongings. Binders with plastic sleeves can be used to store CDs, while small baskets can contain video games.

The same technique can be applied to clothing and shoes. A closet that functions best for a child has plenty of shelves that can be adjusted to his level or baskets that can simply be set on the floor. Although rods should also be included, don't expect young children to hang up clothes without assistance.

And don't forget homework. Avoid a pileup of book bags, papers, pencils, and other study supplies at the kitchen table by creating a dedicated workspace in your child's room.

◄ ROOMS EXCLUSIVELY DEVOTED TO THE ACTIVITIES OF CHILDREN don't have to be chaotic. Here, open shelving and closed storage units provide ample space for organizing supplies such as computer paper, reference books, and art materials. At the same time, two desks clearly define work and arts-and-crafts areas, keeping like-supplies contained in the appropriate space.

Bedrooms

KIDS' BEDROOMS OFTEN WEAR MULTIPLE HATS, operating as a playroom, study area, and sleeping space. Given the many functions that these rooms perform, some chaos can be expected, but too much can make it difficult for even the most spacious rooms to perform any one purpose well. The solution, short of moving one or two of the activities to another area of the house, is organizing the space to meet your child's many needs. Improving the room's storage by adding a flexible shelving system along one wall can easily help you accomplish this goal. This would free up valuable floor space so your child has room to play or so you have a place to add a small table for homework or craft projects. Similarly, lofting an older child's bed can afford you the space required to add a desk below, thus creating a secluded study area. In either case, flexibility and efficient storage are the keys to creating a multifunctional space.

▲ IF YOUR CHILD'S ROOM lacks sufficient closet space, create a small freestanding storage space using ready-to-assemble cabinetry from a home center. Covering two facing pantry-style cabinets with a piece of painted plywood formed this enclosed area. A simple hinged door gives the unit a finished look and hides everything inside from sight.

◄ THE BED IN THIS ROOM is framed with a wall of built-in shelves that provide easy-access storage for toys and books. Those shelves that aren't within the child's reach are used to display breakable items. The empty space over the bed is perfect for showcasing a child's work of art.

◀ EVERY KID LIKES TO HAVE her artwork and other fun stuff in her bedroom. These simple shelves are high enough on the wall to keep little fingers away from breakables but allow for an organized display of cherished mementos and artwork.

▲ HANGERS ARE DIFFICULT for little hands to use. To make a kid-friendly closet, use hanging bags with clear pockets. This way kids only have to tuck things inside and contents are easily identified.

THE PROS KNOW

Take advantage of the empty space below your child's bed. Measure the area, noting not only depth and width but also height. Then store appropriately sized containers such as baskets and shallow bins underneath.

◀ PULL OUT BINS, like this one, installed no more than 36 in. from the floor make it easy for a child to store dirty clothes.

Space-Saving Beds

In spall spaces, like a child's bedroom, it is particularly important that space is used efficiently. And if your child's room is like most, the bed is probably the one furniture item that encompasses the largest amount of usable space. To that end, consider a model that has lots of built-in shelves and drawers. Here are a few favorite styles:

- **Loft systems.** These are one of the best solutions for space-starved rooms. Look for configurations that feature shelves, drawers, a desk, and a cupboard and act as a bed, closet, and work center all in one.
- **Trundle beds.** Because the second mattress slides under the primary bed frame, these twin-size designs are a perfect solution for rooms that require, but can't accommodate, two units.
- **Captain's beds.** Lower than a loft but taller than a standard twin, this popular children's bed features a bank of drawers or shelves below the mattress.
- **Headboards.** Think of these kid-friendly beds as modified bookcases with storage for everything from a reading light to reading material.

▲ ONE WAY TO ENSURE that your child's room retains a neat and tidy appearance is to contain all of the storage and function in one area of the room using a single piece of furniture. This custom bed with a built-in dresser serves multiple functions.

▲ SIZE YOUR STORAGE TO FIT what it is you're stowing. For example, when outfitting a nursery, use an armoire rather than a traditional closet. Because its proportions are smaller than most closets, an armoire can perfectly accommodate infant clothing.

▶ PEGBOARD USED in this girl's bedroom is an inexpensive and kid-friendly way to keep dolls, books, and toys organized.

◀ LOOKING FOR AN EASY WAY to organize your child's shoes? Consider a vinyl rack with adjustable bins, like this one, which can be mounted on the inside of most closet doors.

▼ IF YOUR CHILD IS A SPORTS ENTHUSIAST, consider making the collection part of the décor. Here, simple wall-mounted rods keep a selection of sports jerseys and bats in order. A narrow shelf overhead provides space for balls and trophies.

▼ ORGANIZING A SPACE SHARED BY TWO CHILDREN can be a challenge. Here, a custom bunk-bed unit solves that dilemma. It includes two of everything, including the notice boards and reading lights. The built-in shelves are a nice feature for stowing bedtime reading when it's time for lights out.

A Closet That Works

A child's closet can be configured much like your own. Once you take inventory of its contents, shop home centers for hanging rods, wire or wood shelves, and baskets that will fit the space.

When you arrange the closet, consider your child's age and size. To encourage your children to hang up their clothes, rods should be mounted so that they are within reach. If space permits, install two rods—one up high for dress clothes and off-season things and a lower rod for everyday items. Instead of drawers, opt for shelves. They're easier for little ones to use—especially with folded clothing.

Finally, if two children share a closet, divide it in two, then make sorting simple by labeling each child's shelves, baskets, and other storage devices.

► WHEN ARRANGING A NURSERY, think in terms of zones. Here, a changing station was created by simply adding a table with shelves for storing diapers, clothes, and blankets. A shelf with hooks provides a convenient place to hang outfits as well as store essential items such as baby lotion and powder.

THE PROS KNOW

Simplify your child's morning routine by selecting what will be worn to school the night before. Mount a hook inside the closet door and hang the outfit there so come morning, getting dressed is easy.

▶ LOCKER-STYLE CABINETS, like these, are ideal furnishings for rooms shared by two or more kids. Add one for each occupant so they have a private place to stash their personal belongings.

▼ THIS IS THE EPITOME of a well-organized closet, with dedicated spaces for hanging and folded clothes and wall-mounted bins for odd-shaped items. Shoes can fit neatly on the floor.

Creating a Room That Grows

When selecting furnishings for children, avoid investing in major pieces that have a theme. For example, resist the urge to buy your toddler a train-shaped toy chest, even if he's passionate about trains. Interests change and all too soon, your son may be on to race cars or even airplanes. Instead, select a plain painted box that can grow with him from preschool through primary school.

▲ THE RIGHT FURNISHINGS can make organizing a child's belongings easier. This bench provides both a comfortable place to sit as well as easy-to-access storage for shoes and books.

◀ NOT ONLY DOES THIS SMALL BEDROOM have a place for everything, but it's also arranged so that the work area is separate from the sleeping space. To make the most of the tight quarters, clever storage opportunities abound, from the deep drawers below the mattress to the shelves over the bed and desk.

▶ THIS COLORFUL, THEMED ROOM offers lots of storage options, from the shelves for toys and books to the peg rack for hats and a dresser with multiple drawers. The radiator cover with shelf is a bonus.

An Organized Child's Closet

These recommendations from the National Closet Group can be used as a guide in configuring a child's closet.

- Depth: 24 in.
- 26 in. for triple-hung clothing (ages 3 to 5)
- 40 in. for double-hung clothing (ages 6 to 12)
- 55 in. for long garments
- Belt hook: 42 in. from the floor

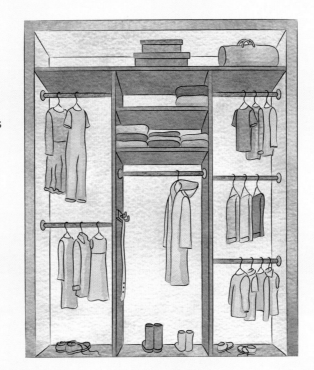

Homework Helpers

IT'S A FACT: ORGANIZATION AND GOOD STUDY HABITS go hand in hand. It's also easier for children to focus on homework when the area they're working in is both orderly and equipped with whatever tools they need. Begin with the work surface. Place a sturdy desk or table (one that's large enough to accommodate a computer and printer) in a part of the house that is removed from the activity and noise of the main living spacezs. If the desk lacks adequate storage for supplies, add a rolling cart with baskets or drawers that can be used to organize paper, pencils, and other necessities. If the desk and computer are to be shared by more than one child, use rolling carts (one for each child) to sort books and supplies. This will allow them to easily transport their belongings when it's their turn to use the desk.

▲ TO MAINTAIN ORDER ON A DESKTOP, group supplies as well as reading materials in colorful containers. To keep the primary work surface clear, consider a desk with a hutch that has shelves located over the work surface or install your own shelving unit near the work surface.

◄ HOMEWORK IS MUCH EASIER TO COMPLETE when a child has a dedicated place to do it. Here, a simple desk made of white laminate provides space for two. The shelf that divides the work surface is both a whimsical and practical addition, providing each child with a conveniently located shelf to stash supplies.

◄ THIS SIMPLE FURNITURE ARRANGEMENT contains everything a child needs to study—a solid work surface, drawers for supplies, and open shelves for reference books.

▲ ORGANIZE THE INSIDE OF A CHILD'S DESK the same way you would your own. Use colorful plastic bins to sort supplies like scissors, pencils, and erasers. Set up hanging files in which to keep school papers. To maintain order, sort through files at the end of each school year, saving only papers of significant importance.

Create an Activity Center

To encourage creativity but control the mess it can leave in its wake, designate an arts-and-crafts area in your home. Doing so will minimize the number of crayons, scissors, and paper scraps you find scattered throughout the house. Here are a few suggestions of what to include:

- A child-size table and set of chairs.
- A bookshelf or cabinet lined with handled storage bins for stashing art supplies.
- An easel and a blackboard.
- Protective gear like smocks and table covers.
- Large containers for stashing cardboard, empty boxes, and other inspirational supplies.
- Jars or plastic containers for paintbrushes, pens, pencils, and chalk.

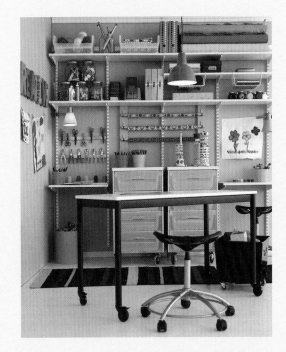

▲ IF YOUR KIDS ENJOY CRAFTS, you'll want a dedicated place for them to produce things. To that end, convert a corner of a basement into a crafter's paradise by lining the walls with adjustable shelves for stowing bulky supplies. Simple see-through plastic drawers can be used to keep smaller supplies tidy.

Saving Memories

Most young children bring home at least one art project a week that winds up on the refrigerator. But what becomes of these masterpieces once they've worn out their welcome in the kitchen? Easy. Place one or two favorites in permanent frames that you hang or display in a specific part of the house. Stash the remainder in a flat file box or cabinet with multiple drawers that are wide enough to easily accommodate oversized art papers. And be sure to select a cabinet with several drawers so you can stash more than a year's worth of work.

▼ CONVERTING THIS BEDROOM ALCOVE into a dedicated study space was simple. The only things needed were a sturdy desk and chair. A shelving unit mounted over the top of the desk provides a convenient place to organize reading and reference materials.

Storing Craft Supplies

Arts and crafts and kids go hand in hand. Here are four inventive ideas for organizing all of the supplies required for a well-stocked art center.

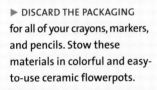

◀ SMALL ITEMS LIKE BUTTONS and beads are best organized by color and style, then stowed in cases normally used for watch or jewelry parts.

▶ DISCARD THE PACKAGING for all of your crayons, markers, and pencils. Stow these materials in colorful and easy-to-use ceramic flowerpots.

◀ FIND A NEW USE for ordinary household equipment. Here, paper-towel holders are used to keep rolls of ribbon and stickers in order.

▶ A SIMPLE SILVERWARE CADDY can be adapted as an easy-to-carry box for scrapbooking supplies like rubber stamps and craft punches.

▲ WHEN POSSIBLE, cordon off an alcove as a dedicated space for a child, even if it's in her bedroom. You'll find that the child is more likely to keep the space neat and tidy if she thinks of it as her own.

Play Spaces

ANY PARENT KNOWS HOW EASY IT IS FOR toys to take over the house. But it's equally easy to make sure they are put away. The secret is providing children with simple but sturdy storage solutions. A plastic bin on wheels, for example, can easily be transported from room to room to gather toys. When all of the items have been collected, the bin can be returned to its designated spot. Or buy baskets with handles and line them up on a low shelf where they're easy for kids to grab and tote to another room in the house.

If your home has a spare room available, establish a playroom that your children can use with their friends. A dedicated space will help contain clutter in one specific area, making it easier for you and your children to keep a handle on their toys. Install a storage system that utilizes both open and closed shelving so there's a place for everything and everything ends up in its proper place.

▲ OPEN BINS are one of the best organizing tools for toys. Why? Because they're easy for little hands to reach into and take things out or put things away.

◄ A STURDY SET OF SHELVES can keep more than a child's personal library in line. It can also be used for getting small toys off the floor. Simply outfit the shelf with baskets sized to fit the space.

THE PROS KNOW

Want your kids to clean up? Make them part of the solution by having them help you select the storage containers that will be used to contain all of their gear. Perhaps they can suggest the colors for the bins or make drawings for the labels that will indicate what's inside.

◄ STYLISH STORAGE doesn't have to be expensive. Here, simple wire shelves have been fitted with a custom fabric cover to make them more suitable for a child's room. Pockets sewn to the outside of the cover are sized to accommodate oversized picture books and art supplies.

▲ OUTFITTING A CLOSET with stackable baskets that rest on the floor makes the space easier for a child to use. Lidded containers, sized to fit the dimensions of the baskets, can further organize the space.

▶ FIND A NEW USE for a standard storage product. Here, an over-the-door shoe caddy keeps Ken, Barbie, and all of their clothes and accessories in order. Pictograph labels make it easy for a young child to understand what's stowed where.

▲ WHEN PLANNING PLAYROOM STORAGE, don't overlook the odd alcove. Here, shallow shelves were built into unused wall space. The bench opens to hide away toys and books, and baskets hold the overflow.

Perfecting Playroom Storage

The first step in bringing order to the playroom is weeding out unwanted or outgrown toys and donating them to charity. Once this has been accomplished, consider a variety of storage containers. Here are a few favorites:

- **Plastic jars.** These are perfect for puzzle pieces and other toys with small parts. Because the jars are clear, identifying the contents is easy.
- **Multicompartment shoe bags.** Hang one on the back of a closet door, and use it to organize stuffed animals and dolls.
- **Metal or plastic buckets.** Fill these with toys, like beach gear, that your child may want to take elsewhere.
- **Baskets and bins.** Because these storage solutions have no lids, they're easy for little ones to fill.
- **Shelves.** Use either freestanding or built-in designs to keep all of the jars, baskets, and storage bins in order.

◀ WHEN PLANNING YOUR CHILD'S playroom, borrow an idea from the garage. Outfit a wall with pegboard, then use it to organize kid-size kitchenware and other toys that are otherwise difficult to store.

▲ THE BEAUTY OF SMALL WOODEN SHELVES, like these, is that they can be placed just about anywhere additional storage is needed. Hang them over a work surface and use them to organize art supplies, or place them next to a favorite chair where they can accommodate a selection of books.

▼ TO ENCOURAGE CLEANUP, every playroom needs at least one storage cart with wheels. Designs with clear plastic bins make it easy for kids to see where things should go.

How to Get Kids to Clean Up

The chances of having a child who doesn't leave toys scattered across the living room are slim. Kids, after all, will be kids. But that doesn't mean you have to clean up after them. The trick: Make them understand at an early age that cleaning can be fun by using the following ideas.

- Make a game out of it. Turn toy cleanup into a game of "I Spy," asking them to locate and put away specific toys.
- Keep it simple. Make it easy for your child to make his own bed by keeping blankets and covers to a minimum.
- Whistle while you work. Lead your children in singing a silly song as they help you tidy up the playroom.

Stackable cubes made of plastic or light-weight wood are one of the best shelving storage options for small children because they are simple to set up and rearrange.

▲ EVERY PLAYROOM SHOULD BE EQUIPPED with open containers like this mesh folding crate. Lined up against a wall, they simplify the cleanup process to one that involves little more than tossing toys in the appropriate container. And because the containers are not opaque, kids can easily find what they're looking for.

▶ WHEN CHOOSING A STORAGE SYSTEM for your child's toys, look for one that can grow in size. Here, stacked cubes, which are small and lightweight, can easily be reconfigured and added to as storage needs change.

▲ KEEPING TRACK OF SMALL ITEMS like game and puzzle pieces can be difficult, especially if a box breaks down. Avoid losing these parts by storing them in small plastic containers, which will fit in standard dresser drawers for easy storage. For a low-tech version, use empty egg crates, shallow cardboard boxes, or silverware storage trays.

▲ BECAUSE IT'S OPEN and easy to dig through, a wheeled basket, like this, is ideal for storing an abundance of dress up clothes, toys, or even shoes.

▶ KEEP BOOKS, ESPECIALLY THOSE FROM THE LIBRARY, on a dedicated shelf. Not only does this prevent them from getting lost, but it also protects them from damage that could result if they were left on the floor. To make sure library books are returned on time, attach a list with their due dates above one of the shelves.

7

Workspaces

Utilitarian spaces seldom receive the attention they deserve—an ironic twist of fate when you consider that the rooms falling into this category, like a home office, laundry room, and garage, are some of the hardest-working areas in our homes. For many families, the one thing that makes organizing these areas so difficult is the simple fact that they're often not self-contained rooms but shared spaces—the laundry room that resides in a corner by the back door or the home office located in a corner in the kitchen.

In places like these, storage systems might be haphazardly thrown together, if they exist at all. To fix the problem, you don't need elaborate, expensive solutions. But you do need to make efficient use of the space for the stuff you want to store now—and in the future. With a little forethought and creativity, you can convert these humdrum areas of the home into efficient spaces that help make your life run more smoothly.

◀ PROPERLY OUTFITTED, A LAUNDRY ROOM can house more than a washer and dryer. It can also contain all of your household's cleaning gear. Ready-to-assemble cabinets like these are widely available at home centers and discount stores. Remove shelves to accommodate bulky cleaning equipment and supplies.

Home Offices

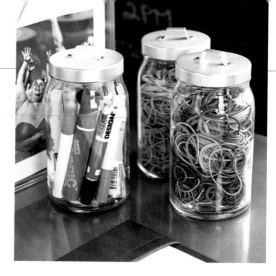

Home offices are no longer just for paying bills and writing letters. Today these busy spaces do triple duty, providing a spot for managing household paperwork, doing homework and activities with the kids, and actually working from home. Of course, the organizing system you adopt here depends largely on the type of space you have. If your office is a separate room, for instance, you'll have more flexibility for utilizing storage units and filing cabinets. However, if it's a cordoned-off corner of the living room, traditional office furniture may not be the best (or most attractive) option. Instead, you may need to devise a more creative solution that encompasses built-ins or some other type of attractive storage. In either case, the key to designing a well-organized office is understanding how you and your family will use the space and how hard it needs to work for you.

▲ SIMPLE GLASS CONTAINERS make standard office supplies like rubber bands, paper clips, and even pens appear more attractive. Plus they're easy to find and get when needed.

▼ WHEN ORGANIZING YOUR HOME OFFICE, don't overlook the wall space above your desktop. Use this area to mount a bulletin board that can be used to post both a calendar and important reminders.

◀ HERE'S AN EASY WAY to maintain a tidy desktop. Use a large tray to contain the small boxes and canisters that hold supplies like paper clips, pencils, and notepads.

Bulletin Board Basics

Not only do bulletin boards make keeping track of appointments and invitations easy, but also they provide a convenient place to post bills and messages. To create a board that complements your office, use one of the following techniques:

- Mount galvanized metal panels over a work area and use decorative magnets.
- Cover a wall with fabric-wrapped cork panels.
- Finish a closet door with magnetic chalkboard paint so you can write directly on it and post reminders.
- Frame a fabric-covered board, then hang it on a wall or rest it on an easel.

▲ INSTEAD OF LITTERING YOUR DESKTOP with an array of plastic containers, look for storage that reflects your personal style. Here, a repurposed card catalog provides plenty of hiding places for stamps, paper clips, rubber bands, and other office essentials.

▲ THE SECRET TO A SUCCESSFUL FILING SYSTEM is to keep on hand only the things you need on a daily basis. Everything else should be packed away in boxes, like these, that can be easily retrieved if their contents are required. Before stowing, label each box with your initials and a description of what's inside.

THE PROS KNOW

If you have extensive files or are placing important documents in deep storage in your attic or basement, create a directory, or list of files, so you know where to find paperwork should you need to retrieve it at a later date.

▲ SIMPLE CANVAS BINS are an easy and attractive way to organize piles of papers. Designate one bin per project or activity and place the bins on shelves so they are out of the way.

◀ SUPPLIES THAT ARE USED REGULARLY should be kept in the open so they're always within easy reach. Here, a collection of old jars and bottles containing an assortment of paint brushes could just as well hold pens and pencils, scissors, rulers, and letter openers.

The Paper Chase

Before you can establish an efficient filing system, you must decide what to keep and what to toss. Begin by gathering all of your paperwork in one place. Then start sorting that one gigantic pile into smaller, more manageable stacks. Here is a quick rundown of what to keep and what to toss.

Keep

- Birth and death certificates
- Health records
- Insurance policies
- Marriage, divorce, adoption, and other official papers
- Mortgage and loan papers (discard 3 years after the loan is paid in full)
- Passports
- Property deeds
- Receipts and warranties for appliances
- Stock and bond certificates
- Tax records (keep business records for seven years; personal records for four years)
- Wills

Discard

- Magazine and newspaper articles and clippings that you haven't referred to in several years
- ATM and deposit slips after they have been recorded in your checkbook
- Bank and credit card statements more than 1 year old
- Business cards you no longer need
- Expired coupons
- Old receipts (unless you itemize your taxes)
- Pay stubs at the end of the calendar year and after you have completed your taxes

▲ WHEN STORING OFFICE DOCUMENTS, consider utilizing clear plastic bins so that contents are clearly visible. Storing the bins on glide-out shelves, normally used in kitchens, makes finding what you need even easier since you don't have to pull out the box and set it down.

▲ KEEP TABS ON EXPENDITURES and save time preparing your taxes by sorting your receipts on a weekly basis. A small box with tabs or an accordion file will do the trick.

◀ YOU DON'T NEED a dedicated room in order to have a well-ordered workspace. This clever computer station is actually in a kitchen. When not in use, the computer, which resides on a pullout shelf, disappears into a cabinet.

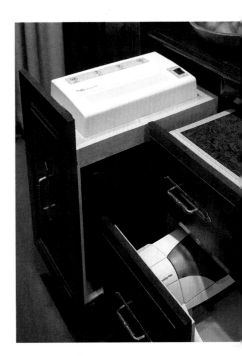

▲ ORGANIZATIONAL TOOLS designed to bring order to other parts of your house can also be used to organize your office. Here, kitchen-style cabinet pullouts allow the printer, fax, and hard drive to be hidden when not in use.

Alternative Offices

If you don't have a separate room to use as an office, consider one of the following options:

- **Armoire.** Look for a unit that has already been outfitted with a fold-down writing surface and keyboard tray, or find a unit at a flea market with a deep interior that can be easily adapted.
- **Reach-in closet.** Remove the rod and any lower shelves. Then add a file cabinet and a piece of wood that has been cut to fit the closet's width and depth. If needed, add shelves over the work surface to provide storage for books and file boxes. Bonus: When you're finished working, you can just shut the door.
- **Folding screen.** Cordon off a corner in the living room or another shared space and use this to hide a desk and shelves.

▲ CONVERTING AN UNUSED CLOSET into a home office is easy. Simply outfit the space with a simple desk and shelves sized to hold baskets or file boxes. Have an electrician add an outlet or two so there's a place to plug in a computer and reading lamp.

▼ IF YOUR OFFICE is in the kitchen, make sure that it's well out of the way of the primary cooking zone. Also make sure there's dedicated counter space for you to work at and a couple of shelves and drawers for storing supplies.

▲ COMPUTER ARMOIRES are an ideal office solution when space is tight. Just make sure that the armoire you choose is configured with a shelving system that can accommodate your needs. Another idea: Select an empty armoire and have a carpenter create a custom interior that will accommodate all of your office gear.

▶ ONE WAY TO ENSURE your desk stays clear of clutter is to surround the work surface with plenty of built-in cubbies. To maintain order, give each cubby a specific purpose, like mail, bills, and correspondence.

Laundry Rooms

I F YOU'RE LIKE MOST PEOPLE, you probably dislike spending time sequestered in the laundry room. After all, let's face it, washing, folding, and ironing clothes are all mundane tasks. But spending time in this bland area of the home is much easier if the space is tidy and orderly. To improve your wash-day outlook, break the laundry room down into individual zones organized around specific tasks—in this case, spaces for sorting, washing, folding, and ironing. Then equip each area with the proper tools for the task. Key elements include shelves for storing detergent and other supplies, a utility sink for clothing that needs to be washed by hand, a rack or clothesline for drying, and an adequate counter for folding and sorting.

▲ A LAUNDRY ROOM CAN ALSO DOUBLE as a utility space. To convert yours, simply follow this idea and outfit a wall with pegboard. Small S-shaped hooks or simple two-prong brackets will keep mops, brooms, dustpans, and other cleaning essentials well organized and out of the way.

◄ STACKING LAUNDRY EQUIPMENT allows you to convert any corner or closet into a well-ordered space for wash. Look for accessories, like a pullout wall-mounted drying rack, that can easily disappear when not in use.

▲ IF YOUR LAUNDRY AREA DOUBLES as your linen closet, make sure there are plenty of shelves for storing fresh towels and linens away from the cleaning supplies. Stowing front-loading equipment under a laminate or solid-surface counter will aid when folding and sorting.

THE PROS KNOW

Make shelves over or near the washer and dryer open so that it's quick to grab detergent and bleach when doing laundry and easy to see when you're running out of laundry supplies.

To simplify the task of doing laundry, place labeled portable receptacles (either baskets or bags) in each family member's bedroom or bath. When the receptacle is full, the family member can carry it to the laundry room.

▲ THIS LAUNDRY ROOM KEEPS AN ABUNDANCE of supplies neatly hidden. The vertical cabinets hide bulk cleaning supplies and provide a place for fresh towels and linens, while open shelving keeps detergent and other essential supplies within easy reach. A small table offers a nearby surface for sorting and folding clothes.

Contain It

Make your laundry room more appealing by repackaging essential supplies like laundry soap, fabric softener, and clothespins in decorative containers with the contents clearly marked. Utilize the following favorites:

- Lidded glass jars in a variety of shapes and sizes
- Colored glass or plastic bottles
- Stainless-steel kitchen or bathroom canisters
- Vintage cookie jars
- Plastic boxes with colored lids

▲ WOODEN PEGS ARE A HANDSOME WAY to add functionality to any laundry area. Use them to hang clothing items that must be air-dried. In this bright space, the shelf above the pegs is used to keep extra cleaning supplies within easy reach.

▲ THERE'S NO REASON WHY the laundry room can't be attractive. Empty the contents of unsightly detergent boxes into large, lidded glass containers that you can arrange neatly on a shelf.

▲ WHETHER YOUR WASH AREA is large or small, take advantage of what would otherwise be unused space. Here, two rods were installed above a small sink, while hooks were added beside it. Both areas are ideal for hanging items that you don't want to place in the dryer.

Create a Simple Sewing Space

A charming and functional sewing space will make mending clothes feel like less of a chore. Include a wall-mounted rack to keep thread organized and within reach. To keep supplies orderly, utilize mason jars or plastic boxes with built-in dividers for buttons, thimbles, patches, and other small items.

▼ STORING SPOOLS OF THREAD on a wall-mounted rack makes it easier to find the color you need to mend clothing.

▲ EVERY LAUNDRY ROOM should be equipped with hanging space for clothes that can't go in the dryer. Here, the rod was mounted over the sink, a clever move that not only conserves space, but also ensures that water won't drip all over the floor.

▲ IF YOU DON'T HAVE SPACE for a wall-mounted storage system, keep all of your sewing supplies in a basket that's stored on a shelf in the laundry room.

◄ FRONT-LOADING APPLIANCES allow laundry equipment to be stowed under a counter that offers plenty of elbow room for folding. They also make it possible to hide equipment in a hallway closet behind closed doors. Mount wire shelves over the laundry equipment to keep cleaning supplies close at hand.

◄ SIMPLIFY THE SORTING PROCESS by using a separate basket for each family member's laundry. Choose one color for dirty clothes and another for clean. Install a bank of shelves in the laundry room to stow the baskets.

Garages

IN MANY HOMES, THE GARAGE IS A DUMPING GROUND—a jumbled mess of everything that won't fit elsewhere in the house. Besides cars, this includes bikes, lawn equipment, trash cans, and workbenches. Converting this disorganized area into a hardworking, functional space doesn't have to be difficult. You can, for example, reinstall old kitchen cabinets and use them to keep bulk buys in order until they are needed. Pegboard can be added to the walls to hang equipment and tools. You can also take advantage of ceiling space by adding hooks for bikes, canoes, kayaks, and other large sports gear. If shelving is required, home centers and discount stores carry a wide variety of inexpensive wire, metal, and wood designs. The key is corralling large like items and keeping everything else in containers or cabinets that make it easy to identify what's inside.

▲ INSTALL FLOOR-TO-CEILING SHELVING in your garage and soon the space will look as orderly as the rest of your house. Adjustable shelves will allow for maximum flexibility. Use plastic crates to contain smaller items to keep them from spilling onto the floor.

◀ GIVE OLD KITCHEN CABINETS a new lease on life by reusing them in a garage workshop. Set an old sturdy door (or buy an inexpensive one at your local home center) atop base cabinets to create a workbench. Use wall cabinets and pegboard to organize tools, nails, screws, and other hardware supplies.

◀ WALL-MOUNTED RACKS, like this one, are ideal space savers in garages that already have difficulty accommodating a car. Because these systems are modular, they can be easily altered as storage needs change.

▼ STACKING BINS, like these, can bring order to a garage that also doubles as a mudroom. Use them for shoes, umbrellas and other items that would otherwise end up in the way.

▶ PEGBOARD IS PERFECT for keeping tools organized and handy. Group tools by function and keep those most frequently used at eye level.

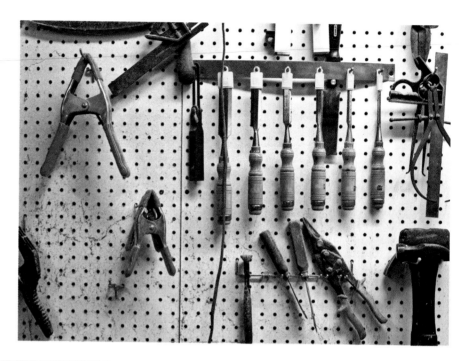

▼ THERE'S NO EXCUSE for a messy garage—especially when you consider all of the organizing systems available today. Wall-mounted rack systems work wonders when it comes to getting ladders and wheelbarrows out the way. Locking cabinets should be used to keep cleaning supplies, paints, and other materials away from kids.

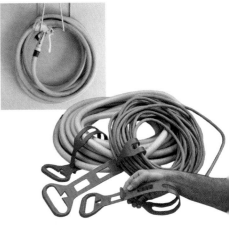

▲ HOOKS OF ALL KINDS can be hung on the garage wall to help keep cords, ropes, and hoses from being a coiled mess on the floor.

▲ WHEN IT COMES TO CONVERTING THE GARAGE, divide the space into zones. Allocate one area for sports equipment, and outfit it with ready-to-assemble cabinets available at home centers. A horizontal rack will keep hard-to-contain items like balls in place; a storage bench allows a place to sit while changing shoes.

▲ CEILING-MOUNTED RACKS, like these, help you maximize storage. Use them to organize seasonal gear or items that you don't need access to on a regular basis. Securing bikes to a wall mounted rack system ensures that they don't end up in the way.

Resources

PROFESSIONAL ORGANIZATIONS

American Institute of Architects (AIA)
1735 New York Avenue NW
Washington, DC 20006
www.aia.org
Lists architects who are members of AIA. The website allows you to search for AIA architects in your area.

American Society of Interior Designers (ASID)
608 Massachusetts Avenue NE
Washington, DC 20002
www.asid.org

For names of ASID members in your area, go to the referral website: www.interiors.org

National Association of Professional Organizers (NAPO)
4700 West Lake Avenue
Glenview, IL 60025
www.napo.net
Lists professional organizers who are members of NAPO. Go to the referral section of the site to find a professional organizer in your area.

National Association of the Remodeling Industry (NARI®)
4900 Seminary Road, #3210
Alexandria, VA 22311
(800) 6111-6274
www.nari.org

National Kitchen and Bath Association
687 Willow Grove Street
Hackettstown, NJ 07840
www.nkba.com
Members are kitchen and bath design specialists. The website has projects, remodeling tips, and lists design guidelines.

CONTAINERS AND ORGANIZING SUPPLIES

Bed Bath & Beyond®
(800) 462-3966
www.bedbathandbeyond.com
A wide range of affordable storage and organizing solutions for all areas of the home.

Broadway Panhandler
477 Broome Street
New York, NY 10013
(866) 266-5927
www.broadwaypanhandler.com
Specialty cookware, kitchen supplies, and storage solutions.

Casabella®
(800) 841-4140
www.casabella.com

CD Storehouse
(800) 829-4203
CD storage solutions.

The Container Store®
(888) 266-8246
www.containerstore.com
Closet systems, storage containers, and useful organizing tools.

Exposures®
(800) 222-4947
www.exposuresonline.com
Photo storage materials.

Filofax®
www.filofax.com
Calendars and daily planners.

Freedom Bag®
(877) 573-3366
www.freedombag.com
Makeup, jewelry, and other travel bags.

Frontgate®
(800) 626-6488
www.frontgate.com
Innovative storage solutions for garages, basements, kitchens and other hard-working areas of the home.

Hold Everything®
(800) 421-2264
www.holdeverything.com
Kitchen, bed, bath, and home-office organizing gear.

Levenger®
(800) 544-0880
www.levenger.com
Home office supplies.

Rubbermaid
(888) 895-2110
www.rubbermaid.com
Containers for closets, garages, and basements.

Stacks and Stacks
(800) 761-5222
www.stacksandstacks.com
Shelving and storage solutions.

Tupperware
(800) 366-3800
www.tupperware.com
Food storage.

Umbra
(800) 327-5122
www.umbra.com
Office and bathroom storage.

FURNISHINGS

The Conran Shop
407 East 59th Street
New York, NY 10022
(212) 755-9079
www.conran.com
Functional, modern furnishings for every room of the house.

Crate & Barrel
(800) 996-9960
www.crateandbarrel.com
Wide range of contemporary and modern furnishings for all rooms.

Design Within Reach
(800) 944-2233
www.dwr.com
Cutting-edge furnishings with a functional focus.

Gracious Home
1992 Broadway
New York, NY 10022
(212) 231-7800
www.gracioushome.com
A wide range of decorative and practical storage solutions and other furnishings.

Ikea®
www.ikea.com
Contemporary furnishings and DIY storage solutions for every room of the house.

Kmart™
(866) 562-7848
www.kmart.com
Cleaning supplies and storage solutions for all areas of the home.

Restoration Hardware

www.restorationhardware.com
Vintage-style storage solutions for kitchens, baths, and other hardworking spaces.

Target®

(800) 800-8800
www.target.com
Cleaning supplies and storage solutions for kitchens, baths, basements, and garages.

STORAGE SYSTEMS

California Closets®

www.californiaclosets.com
Customized storage solutions for closets and other areas of the home.

Closet Factory

(310) 715-1000
www.closetfactory.com
Custom closet solutions.

ClosetMaid®

(800) 874-0008
www.closetmaid.com
Storage solutions for every room of the house.

Poliform

(888) 765-4367
www.poliformusa.com
Modern closet solutions.

Rubbermaid

(888) 895-2110
www.rubbermaid.com
DIY closet solutions.

KITCHEN CABINETS

Bulthaup

www.bulthaup.com
Modern kitchen systems.

Knape & Vogt

(616) 459-3311
www.knapeandvogt.com
Organizing accessories for kitchen cabinets.

Kraftmaid

(800) 571-1990
www.kraftmaid.com
Kitchen cabinets stocked with smart organizing solutions.

Rev-A-Shelf®

(800) 626-1126
www.rev-a-shelf.com
Solutions for maximizing cabinet shelf space.

Credits

CHAPTER 1

p. 4: Photo © Eric Roth
p. 6: (bottom) Photo courtesy of The Schulte Corporation; (top) Photo © Eric Roth
p. 7: Photo © Eric Roth
p. 8: Photo by Andy Engel, © The Taunton Press, Inc.
p. 9: (left) Photo by Scott Gibson, © The Taunton Press, Inc.; (top right) Photo by Greg Premru, © The Taunton Press, Inc.
p. 10: Photos © Eric Piasecki
p. 11: Photo by Scott Gibson, © The Taunton Press, Inc.
p 12: Photo © Joshua McHugh; Design by Eileen Kasofsky
p. 13: (top) Photo © Eric Roth; (bottom) Photo © Wendell T. Webber.

CHAPTER 2

p. 14: Photo © Brian Vanden Brink
p 16: (left) Photo © 2005 www.carolynbates.com; (right) Photo © Melabee M. Miller
p. 17: (left) Photo © Wendell T. Webber; (right) Photo © Phillip Ennis; Design by Ronald Bricke
p. 19: (top) Photo © Rob Karosis/www.robkarosis.com; (bottom left) Photo © 2005 www.carolynbates.com; (bottom right) Photo © Robert Perron, photographer
p. 20: (top left & right) Photos © Brian Vanden Brink; (bottom left) Photo © Chipper Hatter
p. 21: (top) Photo © Brian Vanden Brink; (bottom) Photo © Wendell T. Webber
p. 22: (top) Photo © Wendell T. Webber; (bottom) Photo by Karen Tanaka, © The Taunton Press, Inc.
p. 23: (top left) Photo © Phillip Ennis; Design by Joyce Dixon; (top right) Photo by Charles Miller, © The Taunton Press, Inc.; (bottom) Photo © Brian Vanden Brink.

CHAPTER 3

p. 24: Photo © Brian Vanden Brink
p. 26: (top) Photo © Eric Piasecki; (bottom) Photo © Tim Street-Porter
p. 27: (left) Photo © Brian Vanden Brink; (right) Photo © Melabee M. Miller
p. 28: (left) Photo © Tim Street-Porter; (top right) Photo © 2005 www.carolynbates.com; (bottom right) Photo © Mark Samu
p. 29: Photo © Susan Kahn
p.30: (left) Photo © Robert Perron; (right) Photo © 2005 www.carolynbates.com
p. 31: (bottom) Photo by Roe A. Osborn, © The Taunton Press, Inc.; (top left) Photo © 2005 www.carolynbates.com; (top right) Photo © Phillip Ennis; Design by DNA/Dineen Nealy Architects
p. 32: (top left) Photo © Wendell T. Webber; (bottom left) Photo © Brian Vanden Brink; (right) Photo © Melabee M. Miller
p. 33: (top) Photo © Mark Samu; (bottom) Photo © 2005 www.carolynbates.com
p. 34: (left) Photo by Karen Tanaka, © The Taunton Press, Inc.; (top right) Photo by Charles Miller, © The Taunton Press, Inc.; (bottom right) Photo © Robert Perron
p. 35: Photo © Melabee M. Miller
p. 36: (top left) Photo © Robert Perron, photographer; (top right) Photo © Tim Street-Porter; (bottom left) Photo © Eric Piasecki
p. 37: (top) Photo © 2005 www.carolynbates.com; (bottom) Photo © Brian Vanden Brink
p. 38: (left & bottom right) Photos © Brian Vanden Brink; (top right) Photo © Mark Samu
p. 39: (top) Photo © John Gruen; (bottom) Photo © Phillip Ennis; Design by Mojo Stumer, Architects

p. 40: Photo © Tim Street-Porter
p. 41: (left) Photo © Tim Street-Porter; (top right) Photo by Chris Green, © The Taunton Press, Inc.; (bottom right) Photo © Phillip Ennis; Design by JFMP/Jones, Footer, Margeotes Partners, Inc.
p. 42: Photo © Brian Vanden Brink
p. 43: (left) Photo © 2005 www.carolynbates.com; (top right) Photo © Phillip Ennis; Design by Ronald Bricke; (bottom right) Photo © Brian Vanden Brink
p. 44: (left) Photo © Melabee M. Miller; (top) Photo © Rob Karosis/www.robkarosis.com; (center) Photo © Tim Street-Porter; (bottom) Photo © Brian Vanden Brink
p. 45: Photo © Brian Vanden Brink
p. 46: (top left) Photo © Eric Piasecki; (center & right) Photo © Melabee M. Miller; (bottom left) Photo by Roe A. Osborn, © The Taunton Press, Inc.
p. 47: (left) Photo © Mark Samu; (right) Photo © Melabee M. Miller.

CHAPTER 4

p. 48: Photo © Eric Piasecki
p. 50: (top) Photo © Chipper Hatter; (bottom) Photo © Robert Perron, photographer
p. 51: (left) Photo © Tim Street-Porter; (right) Photo © Phillip Ennis; Design by K Design/Fred Kentop
p. 52: Photo © Eric Piasecki
p. 53: (top and bottom left) Photo © Melabee M. Miller; (right: top, center & bottom) Photos © Wendell T. Webber
p. 54: (top left) Photo © Povy Kendal Atchison; (bottom left) Photo © Roger Turk/Northlight Photography, Inc.; (right) Photo © Eric Roth
p. 55: Photo © Eric Roth
p. 56: Photo © Tim Street-Porter
p. 57: (left) Photo © Rob Karosis/www.robkarosis.com; (top right) Photo © Eric Roth; (bot-

tom right) Photo © 2005 www.carolynbates.com
p. 58: (top) Photo © Sandy Agrafiotis, photographer; (bottom) Photo © Eric Piasecki
p. 59: (top) Photo © Norman McGrath; (bottom) Photo © Brian Vanden Brink
p. 60: (left) Photo © davidduncanlivingston.com; (right, top & bottom) Photos © Brian Vanden Brink
p. 61: Photo © Eric Roth.

CHAPTER 5

p. 62: Photo © Tim Street-Porter
p. 64: (left) Photo © Tim Street-Porter; (right) Photo © Brian Vanden Brink
p. 65: Photos © Brian Vanden Brink
p. 66: Photo © Rob Karosis/www.robkarosis.com
p. 67: (left, top & bottom) Photos © Tim Street-Porter; (right) Photo © www.stevevierraphotography.com
p. 68: (left) Photo © Brian Vanden Brink; (right) Photo © Wendell T. Webber
p. 69: Photo © Phillip Ennis; Design by Interior Consultants/Denise Balassi
p. 70: (top) Photo © Mark Samu; (bottom) Photo © Tim Street-Porter
p. 71: (left) Photo © Eric Roth; (right) Photo © Wendell T. Webber
p. 72: (top) Photo © Mark Samu
p. 73: (left) Photo © Wendell T. Webber; (top right) Photo © Melabee M. Miller; (bottom right) Photo © Wendell T. Webber
p. 74: (top left) Photo © Susan Kahn; (bottom left) Photo © Phillip Ennis; Design by KAT Interiors; (right) Photo © Phillip Ennis; Design by BT Designs
p. 75: (left) Photo © Phillip Ennis; Design by Bradley, Klein, Thiergartner; (right) Photo by Phillip Ennis; Design by BT Designs
p. 76: (bottom left) Photo © 2005 www.carolynbates.com;